READING
MUSIC
MADE EASY

mobile
online
in print

Flame Tree
Music
BOOKS · eBOOKS · RESOURCES

Publisher and Creative Director: Nick Wells
Project, design, notation and media integration: Jake Jackson
Website and software: David Neville with Stevens Dumpala and Steve Moulton
Editorial: Laura Bulbeck, Emma Chafer and Esme Chapman

Special thanks to: Jane Ashley, Frances Bodiam, Helen Crust,
Christine Delaborde, Stephen Feather, Sara Robson, Chris Herbert, Polly Prior,
Gail Sharkey, Mike Spender and Birgitta Williams.

Special thanks to Alan Brown for the scales notation

First published 2013 by
FLAME TREE PUBLISHING
6 Melbray Mews
Fulham, London SW6 3NS
United Kingdom
www.flametreepublishing.com

Music information site: www.flametreemusic.com

15 17 16
3 5 7 9 10 8 6 4

The CIP record for this book is available from the British Library.

Jake Jackson is a writer and musician. He has created and contributed to over 20 practical music books,
including *Songwriter's Rhyming Dictionary*, *Play Flamenco* and *Piano and Keyboard Chords*. His music is available
on iTunes, Amazon and Spotify amongst others.

ISBN: 978-0-85775-802-6

Printed in India

READING
MUSIC
MADE EASY

SEE IT • HEAR IT

COMPREHENSIVE SOUND LINKS

JAKE JACKSON

Flame Tree Music

FLAME TREE PUBLISHING

Contents

STEP 1
STEP 2
STEP 3
STEP 4
STEP 5
STEP 6
STEP 7
STEP 8
STEP 9
STEP 10
STEP 11
STEP 12

FREE ACCESS on smartphones, iPhone, Android etc. Use any QR code app to scan this QR code

Or go straight to www.flametreemusic.com to **HEAR** chords, scales, and find more resources

CONTENTS

STEP 1
STEP 2
STEP 3
STEP 4
STEP 5
STEP 6
STEP 7
STEP 8
STEP 9
STEP 10
STEP 11
STEP 12

FREE ACCESS on smartphones, iPhone, Android etc. Use any QR code app to scan this QR code   Or go straight to www.flametreemusic.com to **HEAR** chords, scales, and find more resources

STEP 1
STEP 2
STEP 3
STEP 4
STEP 5
STEP 6
STEP 7
STEP 8
STEP 9
STEP 10
STEP 11
STEP 12

Reading Music
An Introduction

This book is divided into 12 sections. Each spread is direct and simple, designed to help with the constant reminders and repetition necessary for learning music.

Of course, READING MUSIC MADE EASY will be a useful companion for later use when you need a quick and accessible reference to musical terms.

The 12 steps are:

1.   **The Basics** This step introduces you to the basic concepts: the stave (or staff), lines, spaces, ledger lines, clefs and middle C.

2.   **Treble Clef**. This section covers notes above middle C and helps you remember names for notes on lines and spaces.

3.   **The Bass Clef**. This section covers notes below middle C and offers different ways of remembering notes on lines and spaces.

4.   **Notes**. This step shows how long to sound each type of note as you begin to understand about the pulse and time of music.

5.   **Rests**. For every note there is a corresponding rest, because where no notes are played a rest will be inserted.

FREE ACCESS on smartphones, iPhone, Android etc. Use any QR code app to scan this QR code

Or go straight to www.flametreemusic.com to **HEAR** chords, scales, and find more resources

6.   **Time Signatures**. A time signature tells us how many notes and rests will appear in each bar of music, and determines the pulse of the music.

7.   **Accidentals**. These are the black notes on a piano, that sit between the whole, open notes on the white keys.

8.   **Key Signatures**. This step shows you how to identify the key of a piece of music, using flats and sharp signs.

9.   **Scales**. Four scales for each key are provided in ascending and descending patterns, in notation and guitar tab forms.

10.   **Chords from Scales**. Chords can be used to accompany melodies. This step shows you how to identify and construct chords for each major key.

11.   **Symbols & Marks**. A simple reference to the primary marks of expression and dynamic used in music pieces.

12.   **Going Online**. FlameTreeMusic.com offers the next steps for a wider understanding of music, offering sound links, scales, chords and other resources.

Or go straight to www.flametreemusic.com to **HEAR** chords, scales, and find more resources

The Sound Links
A Quick Guide

Requirements: a camera and internet ready smartphone (eg. **iPhone**, any **Android** phone (e.g. **Samsung** Galaxy), **Nokia Lumia**, or **camera-enabled tablet** such as the **iPad** Mini). The best result is achieved using a WIFI connection.

1. Download any **free QR code reader**. An app store search will reveal a great many of these, so obviously it is best to go with the ones with the highest ratings and don't be afraid to try a few before you settle on the one that works best for you. Tapmedia's QR Reader app is good, or ATT Scanner (used below) or QR Media. Some of the free apps have ads, which can be annoying.

FREE ACCESS on smartphones, iPhone, Android etc.
Use any QR code app to scan this QR code

Or go straight to www.flametreemusic.com to
HEAR chords, scales, and find more resources

9

2. On your smartphone, open the app and **scan** the **QR code** at the base of any particular scale page.

3. The QR reader app will take you to a browser, then a specific scale will be displayed on the flametreemusic.com website.

FREE ACCESS on smartphones, iPhone, Android etc.
Use any QR code app to scan this QR code

Or go straight to www.flametreemusic.com to
HEAR chords, scales, and find more resources

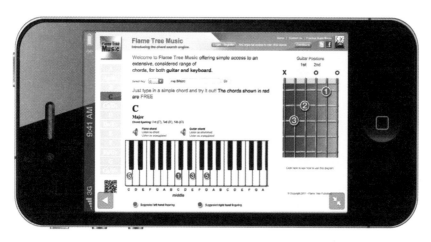

4. Using the usual pinch and zoom techniques, you can focus on four sound options.

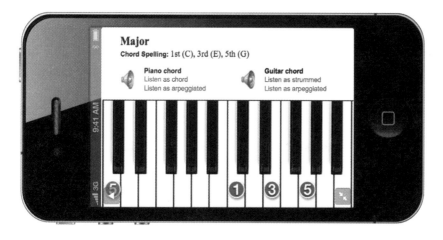

5. Click the sounds! Both piano and guitar audio is provided. This is particularly helpful when you're playing with others.

The QR codes give you direct access to chords and scales. You can access a much wider range of chords if you register and subscribe.

FREE ACCESS on smartphones, iPhone, Android etc. Use any QR code app to scan this QR code

Or go straight to www.flametreemusic.com to **HEAR** chords, scales, and find more resources

The Website
flametreemusic.com

The Flame Tree Music web site is designed to make searching for chords very easy. It complements our range of print publications and offers easy access to chords online and on the move, through tablets, smartphones, desktop computers and books.

1. The site offers access to chord diagrams and finger positions for both the guitar and the piano/keyboard, presenting a wide range of sound options to help develop good listening technique, and to assist you in identifying the chord and each note within it.

2. The site offers 12 **free** chords, those most commonly used in a band setting or in songwriting.

3. A subscription is available for those who would like access to the full range of chords, **50** for **each key**.

FREE ACCESS on smartphones, iPhone, Android etc. Use any QR code app to scan this QR code

Or go straight to www.flametreemusic.com to **HEAR** chords, scales, and find more resources

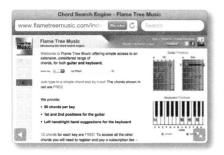

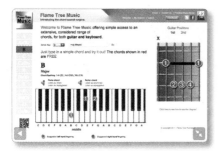

4. Guitar chords are shown with **first** and **second positions**.

5. For the keyboard, **left**- and **right-hand positions** are shown. The keyboard also sounds each note.

6. Choose the key, then the chord name from the drop down menu. Note that the **red chords** are available **free**. Those in blue can be accessed with a subscription.

7. Once you've selected the chord, press **GO** and the details of the chord will be shown, with chord spellings, keyboard and guitar fingerings.

8. Initially, the first position for the guitar is shown. The second position can be selected by clicking the text above the chord diagram.

9. Sounds are provided in four easy-to-understand configurations.

We are constantly developing the web site, so further features will be added, including resources, scales and modes.

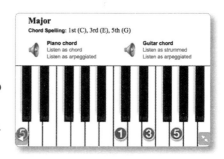

FREE ACCESS on smartphones, iPhone, Android etc.
Use any QR code app to scan this QR code

Or go straight to www.flametreemusic.com to **HEAR** chords, scales, and find more resources

11

**STEP
1**

STEP
2

STEP
3

STEP
4

STEP
5

STEP
6

STEP
7

STEP
8

STEP
9

STEP
10

STEP
11

STEP
12

STEP 1

THE BASICS

Music is created by people singing and
playing a wide variety of instruments.
Writing down and reading the music is
an important part of music-making.

The following pages will introduce you to
the very basic concepts: what is a stave?
What are lines and spaces? What are
ledger lines and clefs?

This section closes with the note called
middle C, the understanding of which
will give you a solid foundation for
the rest of the book.

STEP
1

STEP
2

STEP
3

STEP
4

STEP
5

STEP
6

STEP
7

STEP
8

STEP
9

STEP
10

STEP
11

STEP
12

Stave or Staff

These five lines make up the stave (sometimes called staff).

The stave is the backbone to the body of the music, it holds the **notes** and the

rests and the various **symbols** that tell you how to play loudly or softly, when

to repeat and when to stop.

The stave allows us to indicate **pitch**, whether a sound is high or low.

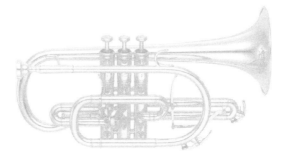

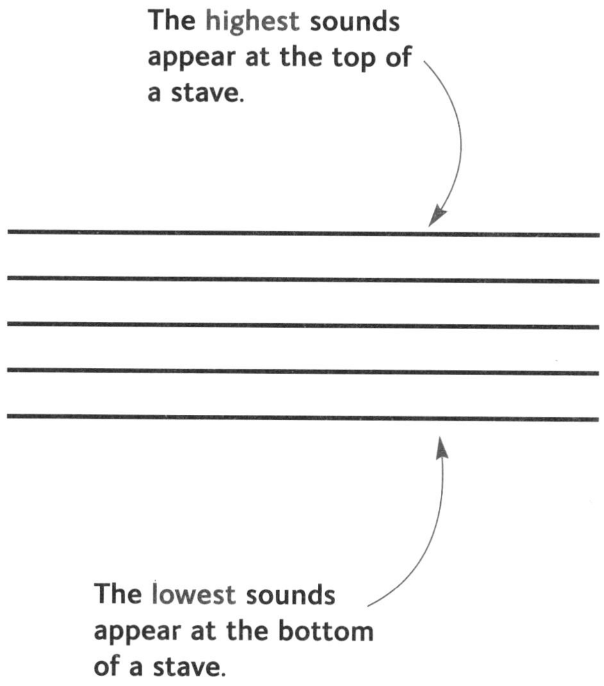

STEP
1

STEP
2

STEP
3

STEP
4

STEP
5

STEP
6

STEP
7

STEP
8

STEP
9

STEP
10

STEP
11

STEP
12

The highest sounds
appear at the top of
a stave.

The lowest sounds
appear at the bottom
of a stave.

STEP 1

STEP 2

STEP 3

STEP 4

STEP 5

STEP 6

STEP 7

STEP 8

STEP 9

STEP 10

STEP 11

STEP 12

Lines

The stave is always made up of five lines. Notes can be written on the lines or the spaces.

Each line on a stave represents a particular musical note, although which note depends on which **clef** is shown at the beginning of the music (clefs are covered on pages 24–29).

It is worth noting that the lines also show the music **moving** in time from **start** to **finish**, and should always be read from **left** to **right**.

STEP
1

STEP
2

STEP
3

STEP
4

STEP
5

STEP
6

STEP
7

STEP
8

STEP
9

STEP
10

STEP
11

STEP
12

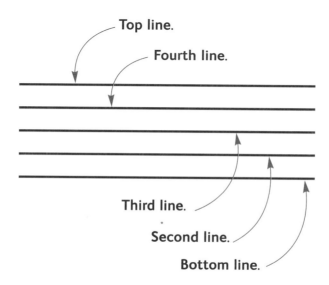

Top line.

Fourth line.

Third line.

Second line.

Bottom line.

FREE ACCESS on smartphones, iPhone, Android etc.
Use any QR code app to scan this QR code

Or go straight to www.flametreemusic.com to
HEAR chords, scales, and find more resources

17

STEP
1

STEP
2

STEP
3

STEP
4

STEP
5

STEP
6

STEP
7

STEP
8

STEP
9

STEP
10

STEP
11

STEP
12

Spaces

Between the five lines there are four spaces. Notes can be placed in these spaces.

The **higher** the **space** in the stave, the **higher** the **note**.

Notes can be placed on **both** the lines and the spaces.

There are spaces **above** and **below** the stave. These can also hold notes.

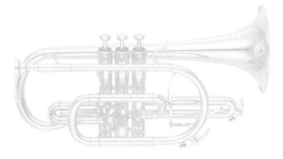

FREE ACCESS on smartphones, iPhone, Android etc.
Use any QR code app to scan this QR code

Or go straight to www.flametreemusic.com to
HEAR chords, scales, and find more resources

18

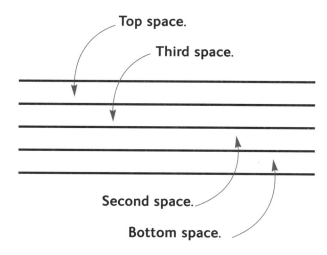

Top space.

Third space.

Second space.

Bottom space.

FREE ACCESS on smartphones, iPhone, Android etc.
Use any QR code app to scan this QR code

19

Or go straight to www.flametreemusic.com to
HEAR chords, scales, and find more resources

STEP
1

STEP
2

STEP
3

STEP
4

STEP
5

STEP
6

STEP
7

STEP
8

STEP
9

STEP
10

STEP
11

STEP
12

STEP
1

STEP
2

STEP
3

STEP
4

STEP
5

STEP
6

STEP
7

STEP
8

STEP
9

STEP
10

STEP
11

STEP
12

Ledger Lines

Often you will see music with small lines written above or below the main part of the stave.

These are called **ledger lines**.

Ledger lines are only used when a note is written in a **space** or on a **line** where the note is higher or lower than those on the main part of the stave.

Ledger lines are written at equal distances from the main lines.

FREE ACCESS on smartphones, iPhone, Android etc. Use any QR code app to scan this QR code   Or go straight to www.flametreemusic.com to **HEAR** chords, scales, and find more resources

20

STEP 2
STEP 3
STEP 4
STEP 5
STEP 6
STEP 7
STEP 8
STEP 9
STEP 10
STEP 11
STEP 12

Notes higher than the stave can appear here.

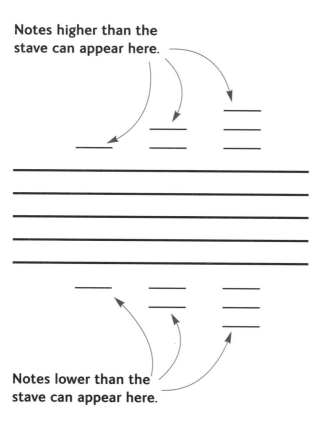

Notes lower than the stave can appear here.

STEP
1

STEP 2
STEP 3
STEP 4
STEP 5
STEP 6
STEP 7
STEP 8
STEP 9
STEP 10
STEP 11
STEP 12

The Bars

When you look at music you will normally see a series of vertical lines placed at intervals along the stave.

These are called **bar lines**. The area between each bar line is called a **bar**. Sometimes these are called **measures**.

Written music, called **notation**, is grouped into bars to provide structure to the notes, to make it easier to follow, and to show the **beat** of the music.

The **first bar** on each stave on a page of music always carries a **clef** symbol in place of the first bar line.

STEP
1

These are bars.

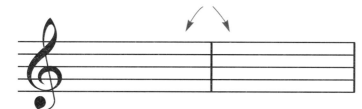

These are bar lines.

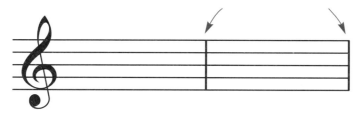

This is a treble clef.

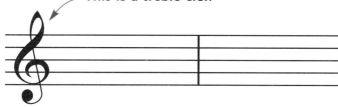

STEP 1

STEP 2

STEP 3

STEP 4

STEP 5

STEP 6

STEP 7

STEP 8

STEP 9

STEP 10

STEP 11

STEP 12

Introducing the Treble Clef

A clef symbol is written at the beginning of a piece of music, and at the beginning, on the left side, of every stave.

The **treble clef** is used for instruments that sound higher, usually above **middle C**. The treble clef always **curls** around the **second line** from the bottom of the stave.

Instruments that commonly use the treble clef are the violin, guitar, treble recorder, saxophone, trumpet and the right hand on a piano.

Children's and female **voices** use the treble clef.

STEP
1

The curl of the treble clef wraps around the second line up from the bottom line.

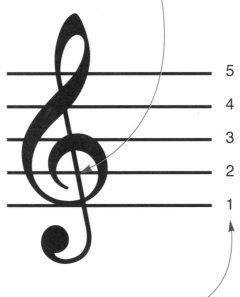

5

4

3

2

1

Numbered from the bottom line upwards.

FREE ACCESS on smartphones, iPhone, Android etc. Use any QR code app to scan this QR code Or go straight to www.flametreemusic.com to **HEAR** chords, scales, and find more resources

25

STEP 1

Introducing the Bass Clef

The bass clef is used for instruments and voices which sound lower, especially those that provide the bass sounds in a piece.

The bass clef is always written so that the two dots sit either side of the fourth line up from the bottom of the stave.

Instruments that commonly use the bass clef are the cello, bassoon, tuba, bass guitar and the left hand on a piano or any other keyboard instrument, such as an organ.

Male baritone, tenor and bass **voices** use the bass clef.

The two dots of the bass clef sit either side of fourth line up from the bottom line.

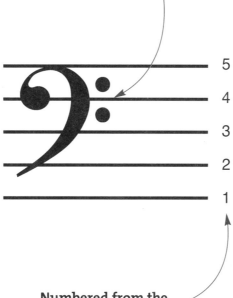

5

4

3

2

1

Numbered from the bottom line upwards.

FREE ACCESS on smartphones, iPhone, Android etc.
Use any QR code app to scan this QR code

Or go straight to www.flametreemusic.com to
HEAR chords, scales, and find more resources

27

STEP
1

STEP
2

STEP
3

STEP
4

STEP
5

STEP
6

STEP
7

STEP
8

STEP
9

STEP
10

STEP
11

STEP
12

The C Clef

Other clefs are occasionally used for different instruments to make the reading of them easier. These include the alto clef and the tenor clef (also called C clefs).

The **alto clef** can be used by the viola. The middle of this clef sits on the line that normally holds the middle C.

The **tenor clef** can be used by the cello, bassoon and trombone. It also sits on the line of the middle C but the five bar lines shift down to provide a space and line below the bottom edge of the clef.

FREE ACCESS on smartphones, iPhone, Android etc. Use any QR code app to scan this QR code

Or go straight to www.flametreemusic.com to **HEAR** chords, scales, and find more resources

28

STEP
1

STEP
2

STEP
3

STEP
4

STEP
5

STEP
6

STEP
7

STEP
8

STEP
9

STEP
10

STEP
11

STEP
12

The middle of the alto clef sits on the line that normally shows middle C.

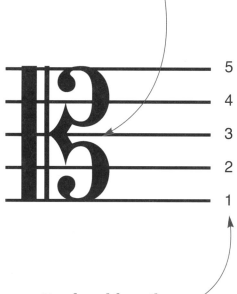

5

4

3

2

1

Numbered from the bottom line upwards.

FREE ACCESS on smartphones, iPhone, Android etc.
Use any QR code app to scan this QR code

Or go straight to www.flametreemusic.com to
HEAR chords, scales, and find more resources

29

Middle C

STEP
2

STEP
3

STEP
4

STEP
5

STEP
6

STEP
7

STEP
8

STEP
9

STEP
10

STEP
11

STEP
12

The note called middle C appears in the middle of the piano.

It is usually the **lowest note** that an instrument using a **treble clef** can play.

Middle C appears on the first ledger line **below** the **treble clef** and the first ledger line **above** the **bass clef**. Middle C sits exactly between the treble and bass clef staves.

To make the reading and writing of notation easier, the gap between the staves of the treble and bass clef is usually stretched out to allow a middle C on **both** staves.

STEP
2

STEP
3

STEP
4

STEP
5

STEP
6

STEP
7

STEP
8

STEP
9

STEP
10

STEP
11

STEP
12

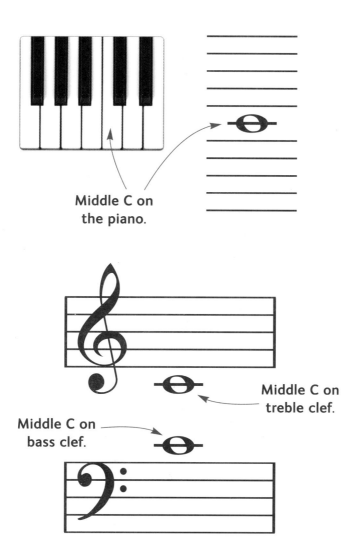

Middle C on
the piano.

Middle C on
treble clef.

Middle C on
bass clef.

FREE ACCESS on smartphones, iPhone, Android etc. Use any QR code app to scan this QR code

Or go straight to www.flametreemusic.com to **HEAR** chords, scales, and find more resources

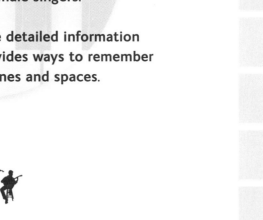

STEP 2

TREBLE CLEF

The treble clef is used for notes above middle C. On the piano this applies generally to the music played with the right hand.

Instruments such as the trumpet, violin and the clarinet also use the treble clef, along with higher voices such as the soprano (or treble) sounds of children and female singers.

This chapter offers more detailed information on the treble clef and provides ways to remember the notes of the lines and spaces.

FREE ACCESS on smartphones, iPhone, Android etc. Use any QR code app to scan this QR code

Or go straight to www.flametreemusic.com to **HEAR** chords, scales, and find more resources

33

STEP 1
STEP 2
STEP 3
STEP 4
STEP 5
STEP 6
STEP 7
STEP 8
STEP 9
STEP 10
STEP 11
STEP 12

Treble Clef Line Notes

A good way to remember the names for those notes that

appear on the lines of the treble clef is to use a mnemonic to

remind you:

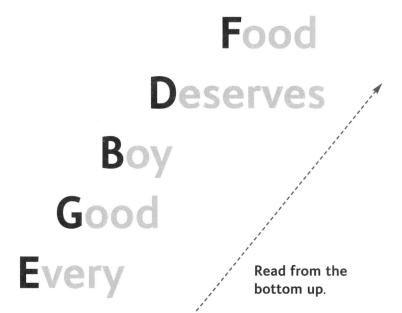

Food

Deserves

Boy

Good

Every

Read from the
bottom up.

STEP 1

STEP 2

STEP 3

STEP 4

STEP 5

STEP 6

STEP 7

STEP 8

STEP 9

STEP 10

STEP 11

STEP 12

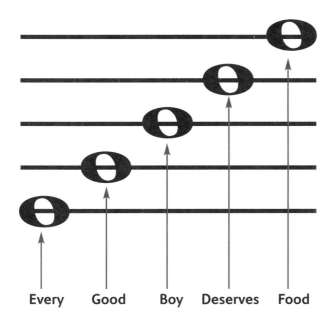

Every Good Boy Deserves Food

FREE ACCESS on smartphones, iPhone, Android etc. Use any QR code app to scan this QR code

Or go straight to www.flametreemusic.com to **HEAR** chords, scales, and find more resources

35

Treble Clef Line Notes on Keyboard

STEP 1
STEP 2
STEP 3
STEP 4
STEP 5
STEP 6
STEP 7
STEP 8
STEP 9
STEP 10
STEP 11
STEP 12

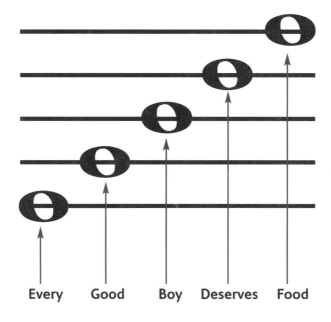

Every   Good   Boy   Deserves   Food

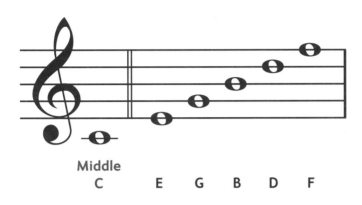

Middle
C   E   G   B   D   F

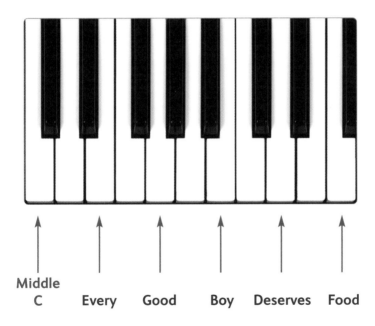

Middle
C   Every   Good   Boy   Deserves   Food

STEP
1

**STEP
2**

STEP
3

STEP
4

STEP
5

STEP
6

STEP
7

STEP
8

STEP
9

STEP
10

STEP
11

STEP
12

Or go straight to www.flametreemusic.com to **HEAR** chords, scales, and find more resources

Treble Clef Line Notes on Guitar

STEP
1

STEP
2

STEP
3

STEP
4

STEP
5

STEP
6

STEP
7

STEP
8

STEP
9

STEP
10

STEP
11

STEP
12

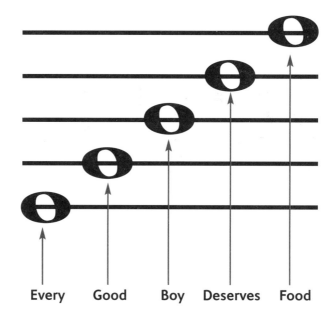

Every   Good   Boy   Deserves   Food

STEP
2

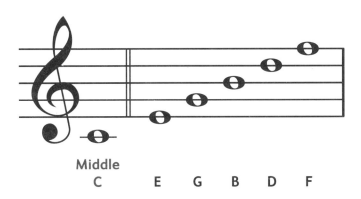

Middle
C   E   G   B   D   F

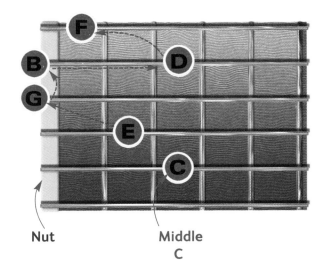

Nut   Middle
C

**The diagram here is from the player's view. Treble clef
line notes on a guitar are spread across the strings.
The notes G and B are shown here on the open strings.**

STEP 1
STEP 2
STEP 3
STEP 4
STEP 5
STEP 6
STEP 7
STEP 8
STEP 9
STEP 10
STEP 11
STEP 12

Treble Clef Space Notes

You can use a similar method to remember those notes that

appear in the spaces of the treble clef. They spell out a

simple word:

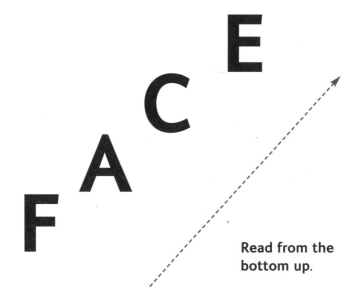

Read from the bottom up.

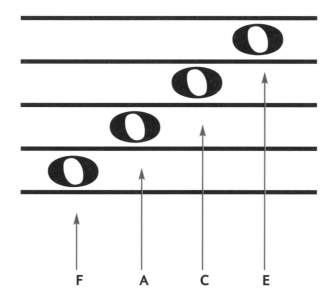

F   A   C   E

Or go straight to www.flametreemusic.com to
HEAR chords, scales, and find more resources

STEP
1

STEP
2

STEP
3

STEP
4

STEP
5

STEP
6

STEP
7

STEP
8

STEP
9

STEP
10

STEP
11

STEP
12

Treble Clef Space Notes on Keyboard

STEP
1

STEP
2

STEP
3

STEP
4

STEP
5

STEP
6

STEP
7

STEP
8

STEP
9

STEP
10

STEP
11

STEP
12

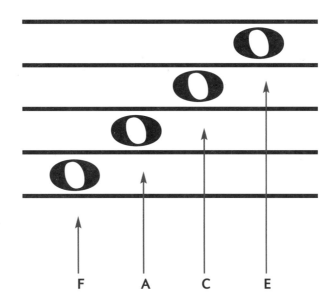

F A C E

STEP 1

STEP 2

STEP 3

STEP 4

STEP 5

STEP 6

STEP 7

STEP 8

STEP 9

STEP 10

STEP 11

STEP 12

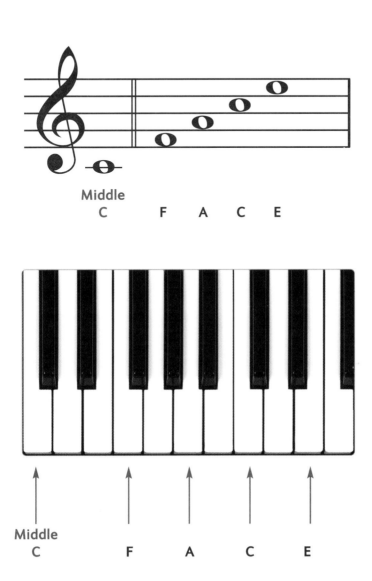

Middle
C   F   A   C   E

Middle
C   F   A   C   E

Or go straight to www.flametreemusic.com to **HEAR** chords, scales, and find more resources

Treble Clef Space Notes on Guitar

STEP 1
STEP 2
STEP 3
STEP 4
STEP 5
STEP 6
STEP 7
STEP 8
STEP 9
STEP 10
STEP 11
STEP 12

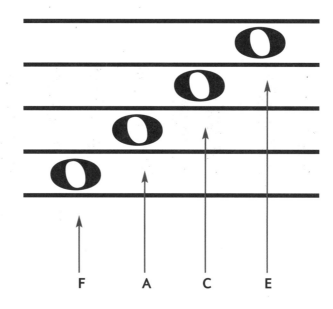

F   A   C   E

Or go straight to www.flametreemusic.com to
HEAR chords, scales, and find more resources

STEP
1

STEP
2

STEP
3

STEP
4

STEP
5

STEP
6

STEP
7

STEP
8

STEP
9

STEP
10

STEP
11

STEP
12

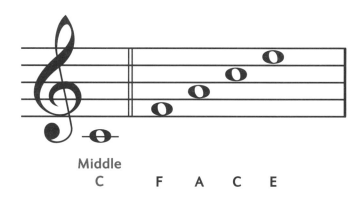

Middle
C   F   A   C   E

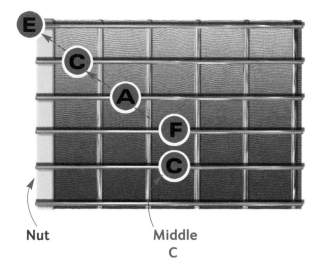

Nut   Middle
C

**Again, the diagram here is from the player's view with
the treble clef open notes played across the strings.
The top note E is shown here on the open string.**

FREE ACCESS on smartphones, iPhone, Android etc.
Use any QR code app to scan this QR code

Or go straight to www.flametreemusic.com to
HEAR chords, scales, and find more resources

45

Octaves

STEP 2

From the previous pages you might have noticed that the note names appear more than once on a stave. For instance, in the treble clef, in the spaces between the lines, the **C** of **F A C E** is **above middle C**, which sits **below** the stave.

This occurs because, in standard western music, there are **7** whole **note names**, from **A** to **G**, which are then repeated.

If you listen to the sound of middle C and the sound of the C above, you will hear that they have the same quality. The **interval** between notes of the same name is called an **octave**. When notes of the same name are played together they create a rich, enhanced sound.

FREE ACCESS on smartphones, iPhone, Android etc.
Use any QR code app to scan this QR code

Or go straight to www.flametreemusic.com to
HEAR chords, scales, and find more resources

The interval between the two C notes is an octave.

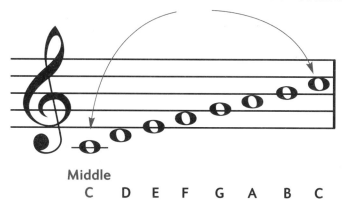

Middle
C   D   E   F   G   A   B   C

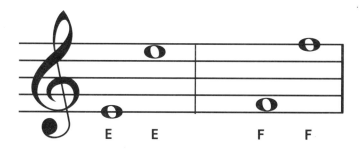

E   E   F   F

Examples of other octaves.

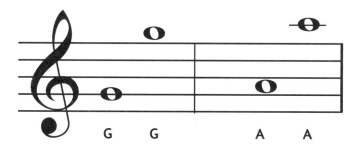

G   G   A   A

FREE ACCESS on smartphones, iPhone, Android etc. Use any QR code app to scan this QR code

Or go straight to www.flametreemusic.com to **HEAR** chords, scales, and find more resources

STEP
1

STEP
2

STEP
3

STEP
4

STEP
5

STEP
6

STEP
7

STEP
8

STEP
9

STEP
10

STEP
11

STEP
12

Notes Below the Treble Clef Stave

It is very useful to know how to work out the names of the notes below middle C.

Remember that the notes start at the bottom, so the **higher** the **position** of the note on the stave, the **higher** the **note**.

Remember also that these notes usually **only** appear on the ledger lines **if** there is **no bass clef**.

However, in piano music, **ledger lines** are sometimes used to signify that the notes should be played by the **right hand**, with the **bass clef** being reserved for the **left hand**.

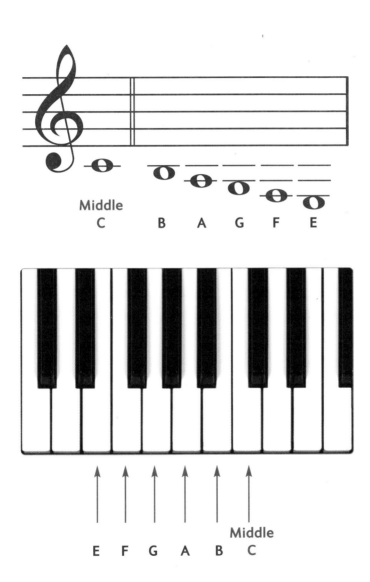

Middle
C   B   A   G   F   E

E   F   G   A   B   Middle C

Or go straight to www.flametreemusic.com to
HEAR chords, scales, and find more resources

STEP
1

STEP
2

STEP
3

STEP
4

STEP
5

STEP
6

STEP
7

STEP
8

STEP
9

STEP
10

STEP
11

STEP
12

Notes Above the Treble Clef Stave

It is also useful to know how to work out the names of the notes above the stave.

Remember that the notes start at the bottom, so the **higher** the **position** of the note on the stave, the **higher** the **note**.

The notes **above** the stave can be worked out in relation to middle C. For instance the **A above** the stave can be called the **second A above** middle C.

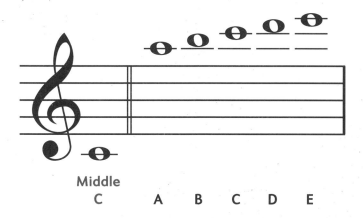

Middle
C A B C D E

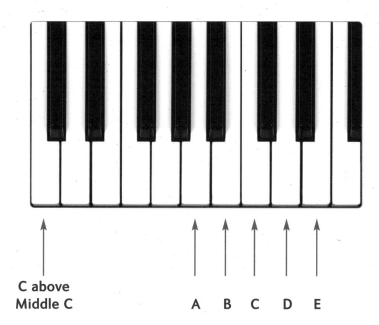

C above
Middle C A B C D E

FREE ACCESS on smartphones, iPhone, Android etc. Use any QR code app to scan this QR code Or go straight to www.flametreemusic.com to **HEAR** chords, scales, and find more resources

STEP 1
STEP 2
STEP 3
STEP 4
STEP 5
STEP 6
STEP 7
STEP 8
STEP 9
STEP 10
STEP 11
STEP 12

STEP 3

BASS CLEF

The bass clef is used for notes below middle C. On the piano this applies generally to the music played with the left hand.

Instruments such as the trombone, tuba and the bass guitar also use the bass clef, along with lower voices such as the tenor and bass sounds of adult male singers.

This chapter offers more detailed information on the bass clef and provides ways to remember the notes on the lines and spaces.

STEP
1

STEP
2

**STEP
3**

STEP
4

STEP
5

STEP
6

STEP
7

STEP
8

STEP
9

STEP
10

STEP
11

STEP
12

FREE ACCESS on smartphones, iPhone, Android etc. Use any QR code app to scan this QR code

Or go straight to www.flametreemusic.com to **HEAR** chords, scales, and find more resources

53

Bass Clef Line Notes

STEP 1
STEP 2

STEP 3

STEP 4
STEP 5
STEP 6
STEP 7
STEP 8
STEP 9
STEP 10
STEP 11
STEP 12

As with the treble clef, a good way to remember the names for those notes that appear on the lines of the bass clef is to use a mnemonic to remind you:

Anything

Forget

Don't

Boys

Good

Read from the bottom up.

STEP
1

STEP
2

STEP
3

STEP
4

STEP
5

STEP
6

STEP
7

STEP
8

STEP
9

STEP
10

STEP
11

STEP
12

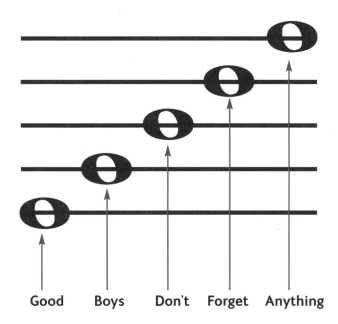

Good   Boys   Don't   Forget   Anything

FREE ACCESS on smartphones, iPhone, Android etc. Use any QR code app to scan this QR code

Or go straight to www.flametreemusic.com to **HEAR** chords, scales, and find more resources

55

Bass Clef Line Notes on Keyboard

STEP
1

STEP
2

STEP
3

STEP
4

STEP
5

STEP
6

STEP
7

STEP
8

STEP
9

STEP
10

STEP
11

STEP
12

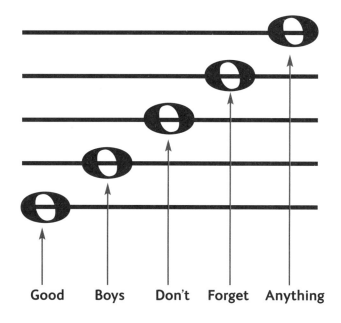

Good   Boys   Don't   Forget   Anything

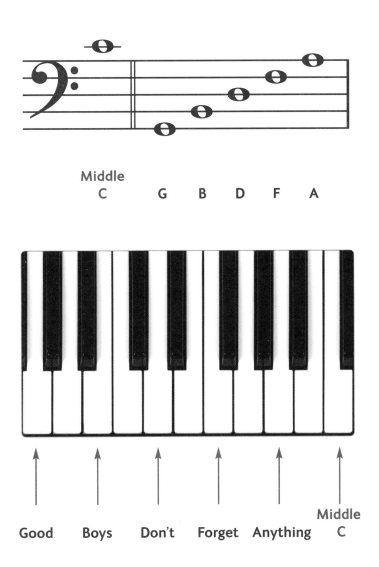

Or go straight to www.flametreemusic.com to **HEAR** chords, scales, and find more resources

STEP 1

STEP 2

STEP 3

STEP 4

STEP 5

STEP 6

STEP 7

STEP 8

STEP 9

STEP 10

STEP 11

STEP 12

Bass Clef Line Notes on Guitar

STEP
1

STEP
2

**STEP
3**

STEP
4

STEP
5

STEP
6

STEP
7

STEP
8

STEP
9

STEP
10

STEP
11

STEP
12

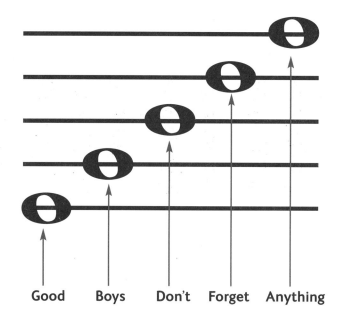

Good   Boys   Don't   Forget   Anything

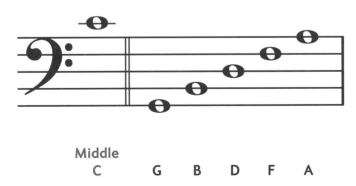

Middle
C   G   B   D   F   A

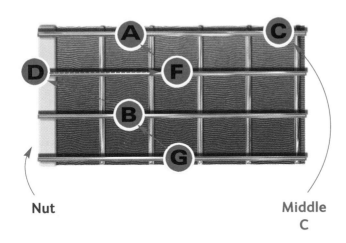

Nut

Middle
C

The diagram here is from the player's view. Bass clef line notes on a bass guitar are spread across the strings. The note D is shown on the open string.

FREE ACCESS on smartphones, iPhone, Android etc. Use any QR code app to scan this QR code

Or go straight to www.flametreemusic.com to **HEAR** chords, scales, and find more resources

STEP 4

STEP 5

STEP 6

STEP 7

STEP 8

STEP 9

STEP 10

STEP 11

STEP 12

Bass Clef
Space Notes

As with the treble clef, a good way to remember the names for those notes that appear on the lines of the bass clef is to use a mnemonic to remind you:

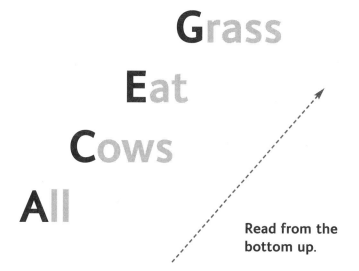

Grass

Eat

Cows

All

Read from the
bottom up.

FREE ACCESS on smartphones, iPhone, Android etc.
Use any QR code app to scan this QR code

Or go straight to www.flametreemusic.com to
HEAR chords, scales, and find more resources

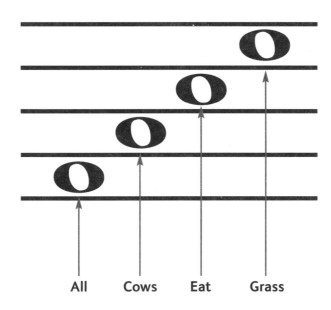

All   **Cows**   **Eat**   **Grass**

STEP
1

STEP
2

**STEP
3**

STEP
4

STEP
5

STEP
6

STEP
7

STEP
8

STEP
9

STEP
10

STEP
11

STEP
12

Or go straight to www.flametreemusic.com to **HEAR** chords, scales, and find more resources

Bass Clef Space Notes on Keyboard

STEP
1

STEP
2

STEP
3

STEP
4

STEP
5

STEP
6

STEP
7

STEP
8

STEP
9

STEP
10

STEP
11

STEP
12

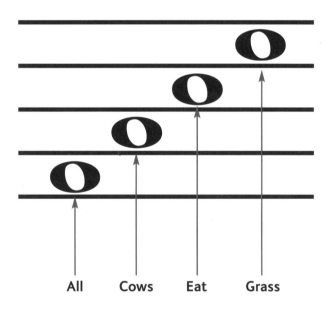

All   Cows   Eat   Grass

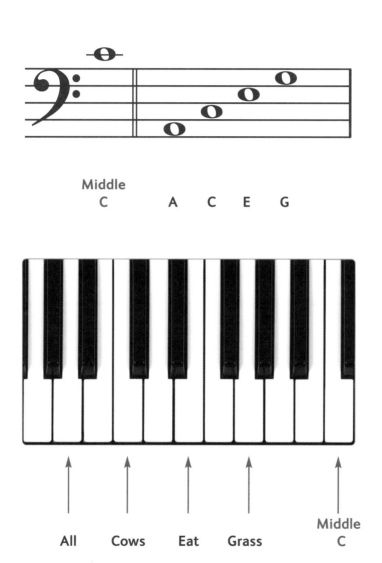

Middle
C   A   C   E   G

All   Cows   Eat   Grass   Middle
C

Or go straight to www.flametreemusic.com to
HEAR chords, scales, and find more resources

STEP
1

STEP
2

**STEP
3**

STEP
4

STEP
5

STEP
6

STEP
7

STEP
8

STEP
9

STEP
10

STEP
11

STEP
12

Bass Clef Space Notes on Guitar

STEP
1

STEP
2

STEP
3

STEP
4

STEP
5

STEP
6

STEP
7

STEP
8

STEP
9

STEP
10

STEP
11

STEP
12

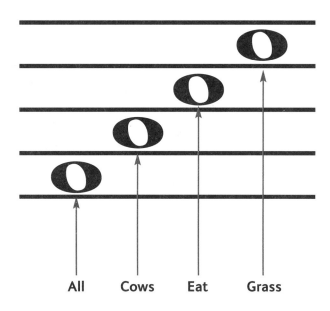

All   Cows   Eat   Grass

FREE ACCESS on smartphones, iPhone, Android etc. Use any QR code app to scan this QR code

Or go straight to www.flametreemusic.com to **HEAR** chords, scales, and find more resources

64

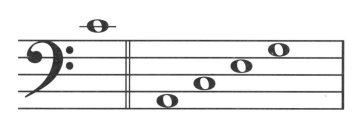

Middle
C   A   C   E   G

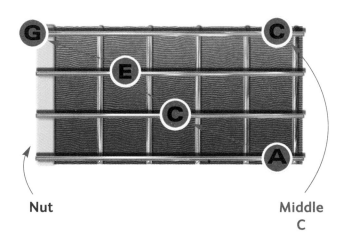

Nut   Middle
C

The diagram here is from the player's view. Bass clef line notes on a bass guitar are spread across the strings. The note G is shown on the open string.

STEP
3

Notes Below the Bass Clef Stave

STEP
1

STEP
2

STEP
3

STEP
4

STEP
5

STEP
6

STEP
7

STEP
8

STEP
9

STEP
10

STEP
11

STEP
12

It is very useful to know how to work out the names of the notes below middle C.

Remember that the notes start at the bottom, so the **lower** the **position** of the note on the stave, the **lower** the **note**.

As a guide, a cello would normally only make notes as low as the C two octaves below middle C.

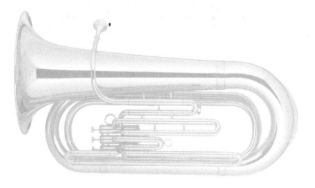

FREE ACCESS on smartphones, iPhone, Android etc. Use any QR code app to scan this QR code

Or go straight to www.flametreemusic.com to **HEAR** chords, scales, and find more resources

66

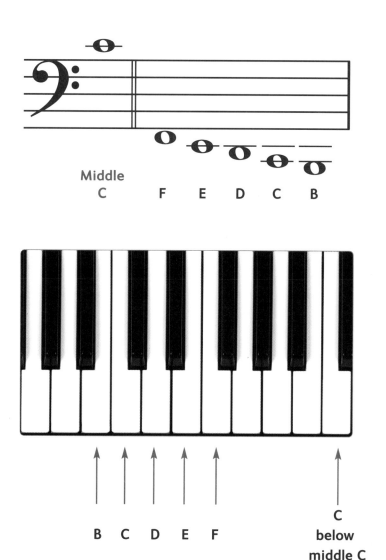

STEP
1

STEP
2

STEP
3

STEP
4

STEP
5

STEP
6

STEP
7

STEP
8

STEP
9

STEP
10

STEP
11

STEP
12

FREE ACCESS on smartphones, iPhone, Android etc. Use any QR code app to scan this QR code

Or go straight to www.flametreemusic.com to **HEAR** chords, scales, and find more resources

67

STEP
1

STEP
2

STEP
3

STEP
4

STEP
5

STEP
6

STEP
7

STEP
8

STEP
9

STEP
10

STEP
11

STEP
12

Notes Above the Bass Clef Stave

It is also useful to know how to work out the names of the notes above the stave.

Remember that the notes start at the bottom, so the **higher** the **position** of the note on the stave, the **higher** the **note**.

The notes **above** the stave can be worked out in relation to middle C.

Remember, the ledger lines only apply where no treble clef is used, or, on the piano, to show that a note should be played with the left hand. The highest note opposite, **G**, is normally the **highest note** played by a double bass or bass guitar.

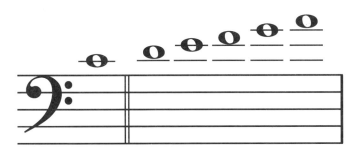

Middle
C   D   E   F   G   A

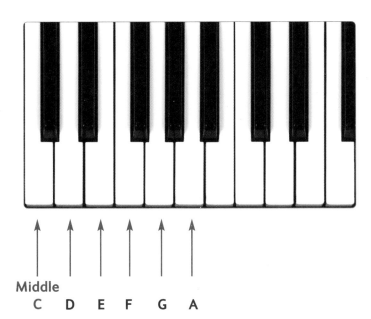

Middle
C   D   E   F   G   A

Or go straight to www.flametreemusic.com to
HEAR chords, scales, and find more resources

STEP
1

STEP
2

**STEP
3**

STEP
4

STEP
5

STEP
6

STEP
7

STEP
8

STEP
9

STEP
10

STEP
11

STEP
12

STEP 4

NOTES

Notes are the main building blocks of
every musical piece.

The position of the note on a particular stave
tells you which note to play.

The look of the note tells you how long to sound
the note and therefore gives you clues about
the pulse of the music and how it relates to the
time signature (*see* page 104).

Notes can be grouped together and must be
replaced by an equivalent rest (*see* page 93) if no
sound is to be played.

FREE ACCESS on smartphones, iPhone, Android etc.
Use any QR code app to scan this QR code

Or go straight to www.flametreemusic.com to
HEAR chords, scales, and find more resources

71

Parts of a Note

STEP
1

STEP
2

STEP
3

STEP
4

STEP
5

STEP
6

STEP
7

STEP
8

STEP
9

STEP
10

STEP
11

STEP
12

Notes are made up of four main parts:

1. The **notehead** is either hollow or filled.

2. The **tail** occurs on notes with shorter lengths – quavers and shorter notes.

3. A **beam** is used when connecting notes of the same value. The shorter the length of the note, the greater the number of beams. A semiquaver has two tails, so it has two beams when connected to other semiquavers.

4. A **dot** is used to add half the length of the note. A quaver without a dot is worth two semiquavers. With a dot this increases to three.

FREE ACCESS on smartphones, iPhone, Android etc. Use any QR code app to scan this QR code

Or go straight to www.flametreemusic.com to **HEAR** chords, scales, and find more resources

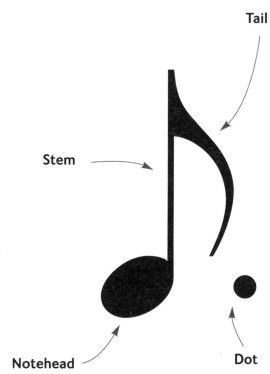

Tail

Stem

Notehead

Dot

Beam

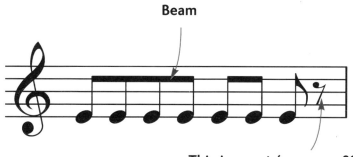

This is a rest (*see* page 93)

FREE ACCESS on smartphones, iPhone, Android etc. Use any QR code app to scan this QR code

Or go straight to www.flametreemusic.com to **HEAR** chords, scales, and find more resources

73

Whole Note/ Semibreve

STEP 1

STEP 2

STEP 3

STEP 4

STEP 5

STEP 6

STEP 7

STEP 8

STEP 9

STEP 10

STEP 11

STEP 12

A semibreve is a note that fills the whole bar, hence the alternative name: whole note.

A semibreve has a **hollow notehead**, with no stem, tail, beams or dots.

A semibreve is equal to two minims, four crotchets or eight quavers.

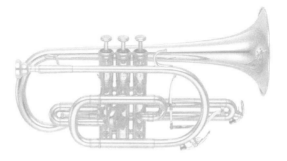

FREE ACCESS on smartphones, iPhone, Android etc. Use any QR code app to scan this QR code

Or go straight to www.flametreemusic.com to **HEAR** chords, scales, and find more resources

75

STEP 1

STEP 2

STEP 3

STEP 4

STEP 5

STEP 6

STEP 7

STEP 8

STEP 9

STEP 10

STEP 11

STEP 12

STEP
1

STEP
2

STEP
3

STEP
4

STEP
5

STEP
6

STEP
7

STEP
8

STEP
9

STEP
10

STEP
11

STEP
12

Half Note/ Minim

A minim is a note that fills half of a whole bar, hence the

alternative name: half note.

A minim has a **hollow notehead** and a stem, but no tail or beams. It can

be dotted.

A semibreve is equal to two crotchets, four quavers or eight semiquavers.

FREE ACCESS on smartphones, iPhone, Android etc.
Use any QR code app to scan this QR code

Or go straight to www.flametreemusic.com to
HEAR chords, scales, and find more resources

FREE ACCESS on smartphones, iPhone, Android etc.
Use any QR code app to scan this QR code

Or go straight to www.flametreemusic.com to
HEAR chords, scales, and find more resources

77

STEP
1

STEP
2

STEP
3

STEP
4

STEP
5

STEP
6

STEP
7

STEP
8

STEP
9

STEP
10

STEP
11

STEP
12

Quarter Note/ Crotchet

STEP
1

STEP
2

STEP
3

**STEP
4**

STEP
5

STEP
6

STEP
7

STEP
8

STEP
9

STEP
10

STEP
11

STEP
12

A crochet is a note that makes up a quarter of the whole bar,

hence the alternative name: quarter note.

A crotchet has a **filled-in notehead** and a stem, but no tail or beams. It can

be dotted.

A crotchet is equal to half a minim, two quavers or four semiquavers.

FREE ACCESS on smartphones, iPhone, Android etc.
Use any QR code app to scan this QR code

Or go straight to www.flametreemusic.com to
HEAR chords, scales, and find more resources

78

STEP
1

STEP
2

STEP
3

**STEP
4**

STEP
5

STEP
6

STEP
7

STEP
8

STEP
9

STEP
10

STEP
11

STEP
12

Eighth Note/ Quaver

A quaver is a note that makes up an eighth of the whole bar,

hence the alternative name: eighth note.

A quaver has a filled-in notehead, a stem, **a tail** and beams. It can be dotted.

A quaver is equal to two semiquavers.

A single quaver is written with its tail, but quavers are more commonly found in

groups with a bar across, to make them easier to read.

This is a quaver rest.

STEP 1
STEP 2
STEP 3
STEP 4
STEP 5
STEP 6
STEP 7
STEP 8
STEP 9
STEP 10
STEP 11
STEP 12

Sixteenth Note/ Semiquaver

STEP
4

A semiquaver is a note that makes up a sixteenth of the whole bar, hence the alternative name: sixteenth note.

A semiquaver has a filled-in notehead, a stem and two tails or double beams.

It can be dotted. A semiquaver is equal to two demisemiquavers.

A semiquaver is written with its tails, but they are often found in groups with a beam across, to make them easier to read. The presence of semiquavers usually indicates a fast passage of music.

There are further, shorter notes, with more tails.

STEP
1

STEP
2

STEP
3

**STEP
4**

STEP
5

STEP
6

STEP
7

STEP
8

STEP
9

STEP
10

STEP
11

STEP
12

FREE ACCESS on smartphones, iPhone, Android etc. Use any QR code app to scan this QR code

Or go straight to www.flametreemusic.com to **HEAR** chords, scales, and find more resources

83

STEP
1

STEP
2

STEP
3

**STEP
4**

STEP
5

STEP
6

STEP
7

STEP
8

STEP
9

STEP
10

STEP
11

STEP
12

Dotted Notes

The length of the sound of a note can be increased by one half, by adding a single dot to the right-hand side of the notehead.

A **dotted minim** has the same musical length as three crotchets, instead of the usual two, so leaving space for a single crotchet or crotchet rest in the example opposite.

A **dotted crochet** has the same musical length as three quavers. A dotted quaver has the same value as three semiquavers.

FREE ACCESS on smartphones, iPhone, Android etc.
Use any QR code app to scan this QR code

Or go straight to www.flametreemusic.com to
HEAR chords, scales, and find more resources

STEP 1

STEP 2

STEP 3

STEP 4

STEP 5

STEP 6

STEP 7

STEP 8

STEP 9

STEP 10

STEP 11

STEP 12

Triplets

**STEP
4**

STEP
5

STEP
6

STEP
7

STEP
8

STEP
9

STEP
10

STEP
11

STEP
12

Triplets are indicated with a 3 above a group of three notes.

Triplets are three identical notes tied together to fill the space of **two** equivalent notes.

Three **crotchets** grouped as a triplet have the same time value as two crotchets, but **sound faster** because the three notes are played.

Three **quavers** grouped as a triplet have the same time value as two quavers, but sound faster because the three quavers are played.

FREE ACCESS on smartphones, iPhone, Android etc.
Use any QR code app to scan this QR code

Or go straight to www.flametreemusic.com to
HEAR chords, scales, and find more resources

**The triplet of quavers above has the same
time value as two quavers below.**

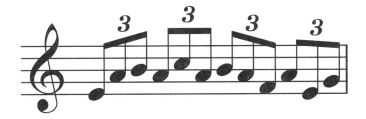

STEP
1

STEP
2

STEP
3

STEP
4

STEP
5

STEP
6

STEP
7

STEP
8

STEP
9

STEP
10

STEP
11

STEP
12

STEP
1

STEP
2

STEP
3

STEP
4

STEP
5

STEP
6

STEP
7

STEP
8

STEP
9

STEP
10

STEP
11

STEP
12

Ties

Ties are curved lines that connect two notes of the same pitch. The line is drawn from notehead to notehead.

Ties are used within a bar to connect two notes where their total value does not have a unique symbol or note. For instance, this is useful for creating the length of a crotchet and a quaver, or a dotted crotchet and a crotchet together.

Ties allow a note to be extended **across** a **bar line**.

Ties within a bar.

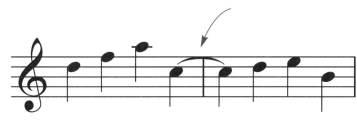

Tie across a bar line.

STEP 1
STEP 2
STEP 3
STEP 4
STEP 5
STEP 6
STEP 7
STEP 8
STEP 9
STEP 10
STEP 11
STEP 12

Slurs

STEP
1

STEP
2

STEP
3

**STEP
4**

STEP
5

STEP
6

STEP
7

STEP
8

STEP
9

STEP
10

STEP
11

STEP
12

Slurs look like ties but they are not the same.

A slur indicates that the music within the start and end points should be

played **smoothly**.

A slur can connect notes of **different** pitches.

A slur can **stretch across** several **bars**.

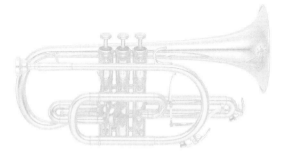

FREE ACCESS on smartphones, iPhone, Android etc.
Use any QR code app to scan this QR code

Or go straight to www.flametreemusic.com to
HEAR chords, scales, and find more resources

90

STEP
1

STEP
2

STEP
3

STEP
4

STEP
5

STEP
6

STEP
7

STEP
8

STEP
9

STEP
10

STEP
11

STEP
12

FREE ACCESS on smartphones, iPhone, Android etc.
Use any QR code app to scan this QR code

Or go straight to www.flametreemusic.com to
HEAR chords, scales, and find more resources

STEP 5

RESTS

For every note there is a corresponding rest.

When looking at a bar of music it is important to realize that each bar must add up to the number of beats set out at the beginning of the piece. Where no notes are to be played, a rest is put in their place to even out the beats.

The look of the rest tells you how long to wait.

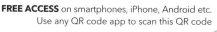
STEP 1
STEP 2
STEP 3
STEP 4
STEP 5
STEP 6
STEP 7
STEP 8
STEP 9
STEP 10
STEP 11
STEP 12

Whole Note/ Semibreve Rest

STEP 1

STEP 2

STEP 3

STEP 4

STEP 5

STEP 6

STEP 7

STEP 8

STEP 9

STEP 10

STEP 11

STEP 12

The semibreve rest sits under the fourth line from the bottom line of the stave.

The semibreve rest has the same length as a **semibreve** note.

The standard musical bar contains four beats. A semibreve rest lasts for a **whole bar** of four beats.

If a bar only has three beats, the semibreve rest fills the whole bar too.

Note   **Rest**

Or go straight to www.flametreemusic.com to
HEAR chords, scales, and find more resources

STEP 1
STEP 2
STEP 3
STEP 4
STEP 5
STEP 6
STEP 7
STEP 8
STEP 9
STEP 10
STEP 11
STEP 12

Half Note/ Minim Rest

The minim rest sits on top of the third line from the bottom line of the stave.

The minim rest has the same length as a half note, or **minim**, note.

The standard musical bar contains four beats.

A minim rest lasts for a **half** a **bar** and so is equal to two beats.

FREE ACCESS on smartphones, iPhone, Android etc. Use any QR code app to scan this QR code

Or go straight to www.flametreemusic.com to **HEAR** chords, scales, and find more resources

96

STEP
1

STEP
2

STEP
3

STEP
4

**STEP
5**

STEP
6

STEP
7

STEP
8

STEP
9

STEP
10

STEP
11

STEP
12

Notes   **Rests**

FREE ACCESS on smartphones, iPhone, Android etc.
Use any QR code app to scan this QR code

Or go straight to www.flametreemusic.com to
HEAR chords, scales, and find more resources

Quarter Note/ Crotchet Rest

The crotchet rest is half the length of the minim rest. It has the same length as a quarter note, or crotchet.

The standard musical bar contains four beats.

A crotchet rest lasts for a **quarter** of a **bar** and so is equal to one beat.

STEP
1

STEP
2

STEP
3

STEP
4

**STEP
5**

STEP
6

STEP
7

STEP
8

STEP
9

STEP
10

STEP
11

STEP
12

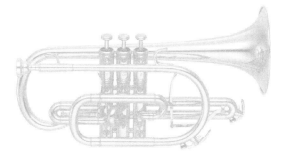

FREE ACCESS on smartphones, iPhone, Android etc.
Use any QR code app to scan this QR code

Or go straight to www.flametreemusic.com to
HEAR chords, scales, and find more resources

98

STEP 1

STEP 2

STEP 3

STEP 4

STEP 5

STEP 6

STEP 7

STEP 8

STEP 9

STEP 10

STEP 11

STEP 12

Notes   **Rests**

Or go straight to www.flametreemusic.com to
HEAR chords, scales, and find more resources

Eighth Note/ Quaver Rest

STEP 1
STEP 2
STEP 3
STEP 4
STEP 5
STEP 6
STEP 7
STEP 8
STEP 9
STEP 10
STEP 11
STEP 12

The quaver rest is half the length of the crotchet rest. It has the same length as an eighth note, or quaver.

The standard musical bar contains four beats.

A quaver rest lasts for an **eighth** of a **bar** and so is equal to half a beat.

FREE ACCESS on smartphones, iPhone, Android etc.
Use any QR code app to scan this QR code

Or go straight to www.flametreemusic.com to **HEAR** chords, scales, and find more resources

100

STEP
1

STEP
2

STEP
3

STEP
4

STEP
5

STEP
6

STEP
7

STEP
8

STEP
9

STEP
10

STEP
11

STEP
12

Notes   Rests

FREE ACCESS on smartphones, iPhone, Android etc.
Use any QR code app to scan this QR code

Or go straight to www.flametreemusic.com to
HEAR chords, scales, and find more resources

101

Sixteenth Note/ Semiquaver Rest

The semiquaver rest is half the length of the quaver rest. It has the same length as a sixteenth note, or semiquaver.

STEP
5

The standard musical bar contains four beats.

A semiquaver rest lasts for a **sixteenth** of a **bar** and so has a quarter of a beat.

FREE ACCESS on smartphones, iPhone, Android etc.
Use any QR code app to scan this QR code

Or go straight to www.flametreemusic.com to
HEAR chords, scales, and find more resources

102

STEP
1

STEP
2

STEP
3

STEP
4

STEP
5

STEP
6

STEP
7

STEP
8

STEP
9

STEP
10

STEP
11

STEP
12

Notes   **Rests**

STEP 6

TIME SIGNATURES

A time signature tells us how many notes and rests will appear in each bar of music.

The time signature determines the pulse of the music, whether it will feel fast or slow.

Time signatures create the framework around which the notes can be written and understood. They organize the sound to help the listener understand what is happening inside the music.

STEP 6

FREE ACCESS on smartphones, iPhone, Android etc. Use any QR code app to scan this QR code

Or go straight to www.flametreemusic.com to **HEAR** chords, scales, and find more resources

105

Two Half Notes Per Bar

The time signature shown with this symbol is two half notes/ minims for each bar.

The **top number** shows that there are **two beats** in every **bar**.

The **bottom** number shows the **length** of each **beat**, in this case **half notes/minims**.

STEP 1
STEP 2
STEP 3
STEP 4
STEP 5
STEP 6
STEP 7
STEP 8
STEP 9
STEP 10
STEP 11
STEP 12

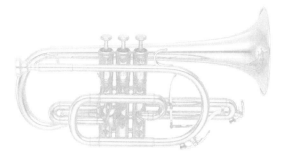

FREE ACCESS on smartphones, iPhone, Android etc.
Use any QR code app to scan this QR code

Or go straight to www.flametreemusic.com to
HEAR chords, scales, and find more resources

106

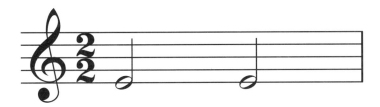

STEP
1

STEP
2

STEP
3

STEP
4

STEP
5

STEP
6

STEP
7

STEP
8

STEP
9

STEP
10

STEP
11

STEP
12

Two Half Notes Per Bar

The time signature shown with this symbol is an alternative to the symbol on page 107.

The C (which is short for **Cut Time**) means **two half notes/minims** for each **bar**.

There are **two beats** in every **bar**, with each of the two beats being **half notes/minims**.

FREE ACCESS on smartphones, iPhone, Android etc.
Use any QR code app to scan this QR code

Or go straight to www.flametreemusic.com to
HEAR chords, scales, and find more resources

108

STEP 1
STEP 2
STEP 3
STEP 4
STEP 5
STEP 6
STEP 7
STEP 8
STEP 9
STEP 10
STEP 11
STEP 12

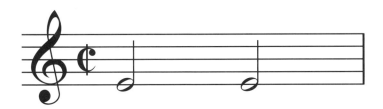

STEP
1

STEP
2

STEP
3

STEP
4

STEP
5

**STEP
6**

STEP
7

STEP
8

STEP
9

STEP
10

STEP
11

STEP
12

Two Quarter Notes Per Bar

The time signature shown with this symbol is two quarter notes/crotchets for each bar.

The **top number** shows that there are **two beats** in every **bar**.

The **bottom** number shows the **length** of each **beat**, in this case **quarter notes/crotchets**.

FREE ACCESS on smartphones, iPhone, Android etc.
Use any QR code app to scan this QR code

Or go straight to www.flametreemusic.com to
HEAR chords, scales, and find more resources

110

STEP
1

STEP
2

STEP
3

STEP
4

STEP
5

STEP
6

STEP
7

STEP
8

STEP
9

STEP
10

STEP
11

STEP
12

FREE ACCESS on smartphones, iPhone, Android etc. Use any QR code app to scan this QR code

Or go straight to www.flametreemusic.com to **HEAR** chords, scales, and find more resources

Three Quarter Notes Per Bar

The time signature shown with this symbol is three quarter notes/crotchets for each bar.

The **top number** shows that there are **three beats** in every **bar**.

The **bottom** number shows the **length** of each **beat**, in this case **quarter notes/crotchets**.

STEP
1

STEP
2

STEP
3

STEP
4

STEP
5

**STEP
6**

STEP
7

STEP
8

STEP
9

STEP
10

STEP
11

STEP
12

FREE ACCESS on smartphones, iPhone, Android etc. Use any QR code app to scan this QR code

Or go straight to www.flametreemusic.com to **HEAR** chords, scales, and find more resources

112

FREE ACCESS on smartphones, iPhone, Android etc. Use any QR code app to scan this QR code

Or go straight to www.flametreemusic.com to **HEAR** chords, scales, and find more resources

STEP 1

STEP 2

STEP 3

STEP 4

STEP 5

STEP 6

STEP 7

STEP 8

STEP 9

STEP 10

STEP 11

STEP 12

Four Quarter Notes Per Bar

The time signature shown with this symbol is four quarter notes/crotchets for each bar.

The **top number** shows that there are **four beats** in every **bar**.

The **bottom** number shows the **length** of each **beat**, in this case **quarter** notes/crotchets.

FREE ACCESS on smartphones, iPhone, Android etc. Use any QR code app to scan this QR code

Or go straight to www.flametreemusic.com to **HEAR** chords, scales, and find more resources

STEP
1

STEP
2

STEP
3

STEP
4

STEP
5

STEP
6

STEP
7

STEP
8

STEP
9

STEP
10

STEP
11

STEP
12

FREE ACCESS on smartphones, iPhone, Android etc.
Use any QR code app to scan this QR code

Or go straight to www.flametreemusic.com to
HEAR chords, scales, and find more resources

STEP 1
STEP 2
STEP 3
STEP 4
STEP 5
STEP 6
STEP 7
STEP 8
STEP 9
STEP 10
STEP 11
STEP 12

Four Quarter Notes Per Bar

The time signature shown with this symbol is an alternative to the symbol on the previous page.

The C (which is short for **Common Time**) means **four quarter notes/crotchets** for each **bar**.

There are **four beats** in every **bar**, with each of the four beats being quarter notes/crotchets.

FREE ACCESS on smartphones, iPhone, Android etc.
Use any QR code app to scan this QR code

Or go straight to www.flametreemusic.com to
HEAR chords, scales, and find more resources

116

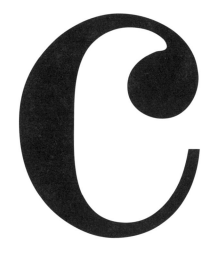

STEP 1

STEP 2

STEP 3

STEP 4

STEP 5

STEP 6

STEP 7

STEP 8

STEP 9

STEP 10

STEP 11

STEP 12

FREE ACCESS on smartphones, iPhone, Android etc. Use any QR code app to scan this QR code

Or go straight to www.flametreemusic.com to **HEAR** chords, scales, and find more resources

Five Quarter Notes Per Bar

STEP
1

STEP
2

STEP
3

STEP
4

STEP
5

STEP
6

STEP
7

STEP
8

STEP
9

STEP
10

STEP
11

STEP
12

The time signature shown with this symbol is five quarter notes/crotchets for each bar.

The **top number** shows that there are **five beats** in every **bar**.

The **bottom** number shows the **length** of each **beat**, in this case, **quarter notes/crotchets**.

FREE ACCESS on smartphones, iPhone, Android etc.
Use any QR code app to scan this QR code

Or go straight to www.flametreemusic.com to
HEAR chords, scales, and find more resources

118

FREE ACCESS on smartphones, iPhone, Android etc.
Use any QR code app to scan this QR code

Or go straight to www.flametreemusic.com to
HEAR chords, scales, and find more resources

119

STEP 1

STEP 2

STEP 3

STEP 4

STEP 5

STEP 6

STEP 7

STEP 8

STEP 9

STEP 10

STEP 11

STEP 12

Six Eighth Notes Per Bar

The time signature shown with this symbol is six eighth notes/quavers for each bar.

The **top number** shows that there are **six beats** in every **bar**.

The **bottom** number shows the **length** of each **beat**, in this case, **eighth notes/quavers**.

In this time signature the six notes are grouped in threes.

FREE ACCESS on smartphones, iPhone, Android etc.
Use any QR code app to scan this QR code

Or go straight to www.flametreemusic.com to
HEAR chords, scales, and find more resources

120

STEP 1
STEP 2
STEP 3
STEP 4
STEP 5
STEP 6
STEP 7
STEP 8
STEP 9
STEP 10
STEP 11
STEP 12

STEP
1

STEP
2

STEP
3

STEP
4

STEP
5

STEP
6

STEP
7

STEP
8

STEP
9

STEP
10

STEP
11

STEP
12

FREE ACCESS on smartphones, iPhone, Android etc.
Use any QR code app to scan this QR code

Or go straight to www.flametreemusic.com to
HEAR chords, scales, and find more resources

STEP 7

ACCIDENTALS

The notes we've covered so far in this book have been natural notes. They are played on the white notes of a piano and have the following names:

A B C D E F G

However, there are notes that sit between some of these whole notes. These are called accidentals and on the piano they are played on the black keys. These notes are half a tone (a semitone) below or above the white notes and are indicated by a flat, sharp or sometimes a natural sign.

FREE ACCESS on smartphones, iPhone, Android etc. Use any QR code app to scan this QR code

Or go straight to www.flametreemusic.com to **HEAR** chords, scales, and find more resources

123

Natural & Accidental Notes on the Keyboard

You can see here how the 12 notes work before they are repeated. For clarity at this stage the diagrams opposite just use sharp signs, although later we will look at flat signs too.

On the piano the **natural notes** appear on the **white** keys, with the **sharp** notes on the **black** keys. The difference in pitch between these and any number of notes is called an **interval**.

You can see that black notes do not appear between E and F or B and C. This begins to show us how a **scale**, which depends on different intervals, might work. We look at this later from page 176.

FREE ACCESS on smartphones, iPhone, Android etc.
Use any QR code app to scan this QR code

Or go straight to www.flametreemusic.com to
HEAR chords, scales, and find more resources

124

STEP 1
STEP 2
STEP 3
STEP 4
STEP 5
STEP 6
STEP 7
STEP 8
STEP 9
STEP 10
STEP 11
STEP 12

C C♯ D D♯ E F F♯ G G♯ A A♯ B

Natural notes on the white keys,
sharp notes on the black keys

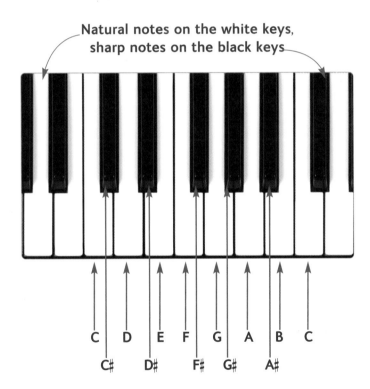

C D E F G A B C

C♯ D♯ F♯ G♯ A♯

FREE ACCESS on smartphones, iPhone, Android etc.
Use any QR code app to scan this QR code

Or go straight to www.flametreemusic.com to
HEAR chords, scales, and find more resources

125

Sharps

STEP
1

STEP
2

STEP
3

STEP
4

STEP
5

STEP
6

**STEP
7**

STEP
8

STEP
9

STEP
10

STEP
11

STEP
12

This is the sharp sign.

It is written to the **left** of a notehead.

A **sharpened** note is half a tone **higher** than the note that is being sharpened.

When a sharp is written in front of a particular note all **subsequent uses**

of that note **in the bar** will also be **sharpened**. From the beginning of the

next bar, the note **reverts** to its previous state.

Sharpened notes are played on the **black** keys of a piano.

FREE ACCESS on smartphones, iPhone, Android etc.
Use any QR code app to scan this QR code

Or go straight to www.flametreemusic.com to
HEAR chords, scales, and find more resources

126

STEP
7

Sharp Notes on the Keyboard

Sharp notes appear on the black keys on the piano. Black keys do not appear between every pair of white keys: there is no black key between B and C, or between E and F.

So B♯ is the **same note** as C.

And E♯ is the **same note** as F.

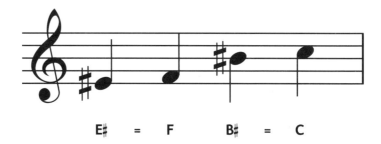

E♯ = F   B♯ = C

STEP 7

FREE ACCESS on smartphones, iPhone, Android etc. Use any QR code app to scan this QR code

Or go straight to www.flametreemusic.com to **HEAR** chords, scales, and find more resources

128

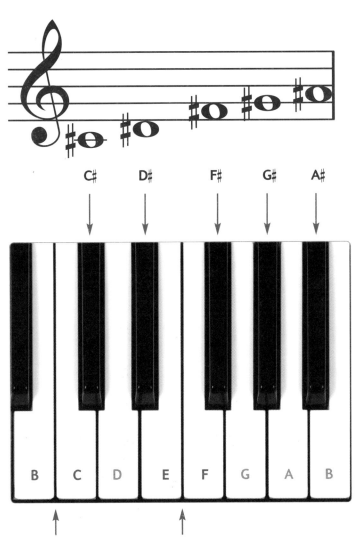

Semitone interval between these notes.

Sharp Notes on the Guitar

On the guitar the frets are organized in half tone intervals so sharp notes appear after their natural note.

The diagram below shows you all the notes in the **first position** on the guitar.

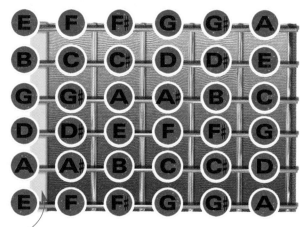

Nut

Player's view. Bass notes at the bottom.

  Or go straight to www.flametreemusic.com to **HEAR** chords, scales, and find more resources

STEP 1
STEP 2
STEP 3
STEP 4
STEP 5
STEP 6
STEP 7
STEP 8
STEP 9
STEP 10
STEP 11
STEP 12

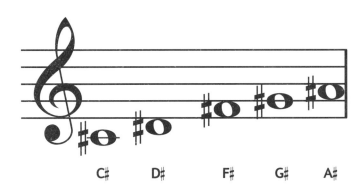

C#   D#   F#   G#   A#

**These are the sharp notes in the octave
above middle C.**

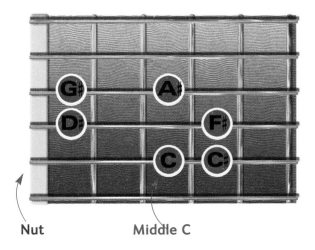

Nut   Middle C

FREE ACCESS on smartphones, iPhone, Android etc.
Use any QR code app to scan this QR code

Or go straight to www.flametreemusic.com to
HEAR chords, scales, and find more resources

131

Flats

This is the flat sign.

It is written to the **left** of a notehead.

A **flattened** note is half a tone **lower** than the note that is being flattened.

**STEP
7**

When a flat is written in front of a particular note all **subsequent uses** of that

note **in the bar** will also be **flattened**. From the beginning of the **next bar**,

the note **reverts** to its previous state.

Flattened notes are played on the **black** keys of a piano

FREE ACCESS on smartphones, iPhone, Android etc.
Use any QR code app to scan this QR code

Or go straight to www.flametreemusic.com to
HEAR chords, scales, and find more resources

132

FREE ACCESS on smartphones, iPhone, Android etc. Use any QR code app to scan this QR code

Or go straight to www.flametreemusic.com to **HEAR** chords, scales, and find more resources

STEP
7

Flat Notes on the Keyboard

Flat notes appear on the black keys on the piano. As you have seen previously, **black** keys do **not** appear between **every** pair of **white** keys: there is **no black key** between **B** and **C**, or **E** and **F**.

So **C♭** is the **same note** as **B**

And **F♭** is the **same note** as **E**.

F♭   =   E   C♭   =   B

STEP 1
STEP 2
STEP 3
STEP 4
STEP 5
STEP 6
STEP 7
STEP 8
STEP 9
STEP 10
STEP 11
STEP 12

FREE ACCESS on smartphones, iPhone, Android etc. Use any QR code app to scan this QR code   Or go straight to www.flametreemusic.com to **HEAR** chords, scales, and find more resources

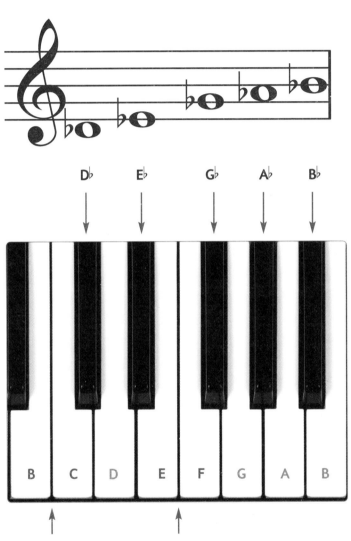

Half note interval between these notes.

Flat Notes on the Guitar

On the guitar the frets are organized in half tone intervals so flat notes appear before their natural note.

The diagram below shows you all the notes in the first position on the guitar, using open strings.

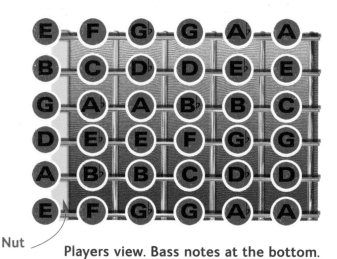

Nut

Players view. Bass notes at the bottom.

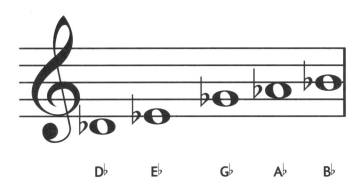

D♭   E♭   G♭   A♭   B♭

These are the flat notes in the octave above middle C.

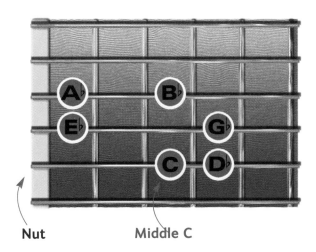

Nut   Middle C

STEP 1
STEP 2
STEP 3
STEP 4
STEP 5
STEP 6
STEP 7
STEP 8
STEP 9
STEP 10
STEP 11
STEP 12

Natural

STEP
1

STEP
2

STEP
3

STEP
4

STEP
5

STEP
6

STEP
7

STEP
8

STEP
9

STEP
10

STEP
11

STEP
12

This is the natural sign.

It is written to the **left** of a notehead.

A natural sign is used to **cancel** the effect of a **sharp** or a **flat** note played previously in the same bar, or present in the key signature (*see* page 144).

Natural notes are played on the **white** keys of a piano.

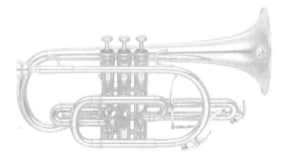

FREE ACCESS on smartphones, iPhone, Android etc. Use any QR code app to scan this QR code

Or go straight to www.flametreemusic.com to **HEAR** chords, scales, and find more resources

138

FREE ACCESS on smartphones, iPhone, Android etc.
Use any QR code app to scan this QR code

Or go straight to www.flametreemusic.com to
HEAR chords, scales, and find more resources

139

STEP
1

STEP
2

STEP
3

STEP
4

STEP
5

STEP
6

**STEP
7**

STEP
8

STEP
9

STEP
10

STEP
11

STEP
12

STEP
1

STEP
2

STEP
3

STEP
4

STEP
5

STEP
6

STEP
7

STEP
8

STEP
9

STEP
10

STEP
11

STEP
12

Natural Notes on the Keyboard

Notes with a natural symbol occur when a particular note has been sharpened or flattened previously in the bar or in the key signature. Once applied, the **natural** symbol for the particular note applies for the rest of bar unless another sharp or flat appears.

A D♯ is a **semitone** higher than D♮.

A D♭ is a **semitone** lower than D♮.

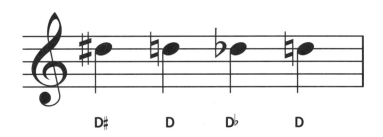

D♯   D   D♭   D

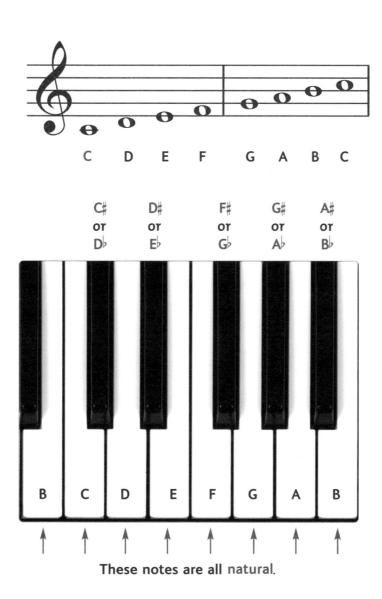

C D E F G A B C

C♯	D♯		F♯	G♯	A♯
or	or		or	or	or
D♭	E♭		G♭	A♭	B♭

B C D E F G A B

These notes are all natural.

STEP 1
STEP 2
STEP 3
STEP 4
STEP 5
STEP 6
STEP 7
STEP 8
STEP 9
STEP 10
STEP 11
STEP 12

Natural Notes on the Guitar

On the guitar the frets are organized in half tone intervals so flat notes appear before their natural note and sharps appear after their natural note. The diagram below shows you all the notes in the first position on the guitar, using open strings.

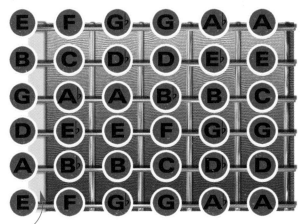

Nut

Player's view. Bass notes at the bottom.

FREE ACCESS on smartphones, iPhone, Android etc. Use any QR code app to scan this QR code

Or go straight to www.flametreemusic.com to **HEAR** chords, scales, and find more resources

STEP 1

STEP 2

STEP 3

STEP 4

STEP 5

STEP 6

STEP 7

STEP 8

STEP 9

STEP 10

STEP 11

STEP 12

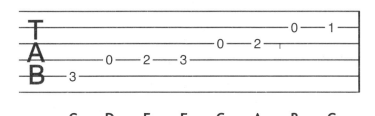

C   D   E   F   G   A   B   C

Some guitarists use tablature (called TAB) instead of staff notation. Notes in TAB are shown on six lines representing the six strings of the guitar.

The low E string is at the bottom and the notes are given the fret number on the appropriate string. The natural notes are shown in TAB above and a guitar diagram below.

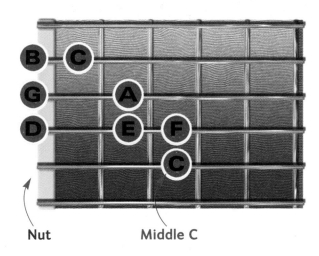

Nut   Middle C

FREE ACCESS on smartphones, iPhone, Android etc. Use any QR code app to scan this QR code

Or go straight to www.flametreemusic.com to **HEAR** chords, scales, and find more resources

143

STEP 8

KEY SIGNATURES

The natural notes above and below middle C are the white keys on a piano. Key signatures allow us to use the black notes, which are the sharps and flats.

A sharp or flat in the key signature indicates that these accidentals should be played each time the note appears. Each key signature contains a different number of either sharps or flats (never both) and makes the music sound distinctive.

A key signature is shown at the start of each stave and is indicated by sharp or flat symbols on note lines or spaces.

STEP
1

STEP
2

STEP
3

STEP
4

STEP
5

STEP
6

STEP
7

**STEP
8**

STEP
9

STEP
10

STEP
11

STEP
12

145

STEP
1

STEP
2

STEP
3

STEP
4

STEP
5

STEP
6

STEP
7

**STEP
8**

STEP
9

STEP
10

STEP
11

STEP
12

Key Signature

No Sharp or Flat

C Major

A Minor

The keys of C major and its relative, A minor,

have no sharps or flats.

FREE ACCESS on smartphones, iPhone, Android etc.
Use any QR code app to scan this QR code

Or go straight to www.flametreemusic.com to
HEAR chords, scales, and find more resources

146

Or go straight to www.flametreemusic.com to **HEAR** chords, scales, and find more resources

STEP 1

STEP 2

STEP 3

STEP 4

STEP 5

STEP 6

STEP 7

STEP 8

STEP 9

STEP 10

STEP 11

STEP 12

STEP 1

STEP 2

STEP 3

STEP 4

STEP 5

STEP 6

STEP 7

STEP 8

STEP 9

STEP 10

STEP 11

STEP 12

Key Signature

1 Sharp

G Major

E Minor

The keys of G major and its relative, E minor,

have one sharp:

FREE ACCESS on smartphones, iPhone, Android etc.
Use any QR code app to scan this QR code

Or go straight to www.flametreemusic.com to
HEAR chords, scales, and find more resources

148

FREE ACCESS on smartphones, iPhone, Android etc. Use any QR code app to scan this QR code

Or go straight to www.flametreemusic.com to **HEAR** chords, scales, and find more resources

STEP 8

STEP
1

STEP
2

STEP
3

STEP
4

STEP
5

STEP
6

STEP
7

**STEP
8**

STEP
9

STEP
10

STEP
11

STEP
12

Key Signature

2 Sharps

D Major

B Minor

The keys of D major and its relative,

B minor, have two sharps:

F♯ C♯

FREE ACCESS on smartphones, iPhone, Android etc. Use any QR code app to scan this QR code

Or go straight to www.flametreemusic.com to **HEAR** chords, scales, and find more resources

FREE ACCESS on smartphones, iPhone, Android etc.
Use any QR code app to scan this QR code

Or go straight to www.flametreemusic.com to
HEAR chords, scales, and find more resources

151

Key Signature

3 Sharps

A Major

F♯ Minor

STEP
8

The keys of A major and its relative,

F♯ minor, have three sharps:

F♯ C♯ G♯

FREE ACCESS on smartphones, iPhone, Android etc.
Use any QR code app to scan this QR code

Or go straight to www.flametreemusic.com to
HEAR chords, scales, and find more resources

153

Key Signature

4 Sharps

E Major

C♯ Minor

The keys of E major and its relative,

C♯ minor, have four sharps:

F♯ C♯ G♯ D♯

FREE ACCESS on smartphones, iPhone, Android etc.
Use any QR code app to scan this QR code

Or go straight to www.flametreemusic.com to
HEAR chords, scales, and find more resources

154

STEP
1

STEP
2

STEP
3

STEP
4

STEP
5

STEP
6

STEP
7

**STEP
8**

STEP
9

STEP
10

STEP
11

STEP
12

STEP
8

Key Signature

5 Sharps

B Major

G♯ Minor

The keys of B major and its relative,

G♯ minor, have five sharps:

F♯ C♯ G♯ D♯ A♯

FREE ACCESS on smartphones, iPhone, Android etc.
Use any QR code app to scan this QR code

Or go straight to www.flametreemusic.com to
HEAR chords, scales, and find more resources

156

STEP
8

STEP
1

STEP
2

STEP
3

STEP
4

STEP
5

STEP
6

STEP
7

STEP
8

STEP
9

STEP
10

STEP
11

STEP
12

Key Signature

6 Sharps

F♯ Major

D♯ Minor

The keys of F♯ major and its relative,

D♯ minor, have six sharps:

F♯ C♯ G♯ D♯ A♯ E♯

FREE ACCESS on smartphones, iPhone, Android etc.
Use any QR code app to scan this QR code

Or go straight to www.flametreemusic.com to
HEAR chords, scales, and find more resources

158

STEP 8

Or go straight to www.flametreemusic.com to **HEAR** chords, scales, and find more resources

Key Signature

7 Sharps

C♯ Major

A♯ Minor

The keys of C♯ major and its relative,

A♯ minor, have seven sharps:

F♯ C♯ G♯ D♯ A♯ E♯ B♯

STEP
1

STEP
2

STEP
3

STEP
4

STEP
5

STEP
6

STEP
7

**STEP
8**

STEP
9

STEP
10

STEP
11

STEP
12

STEP
1

STEP
2

STEP
3

STEP
4

STEP
5

STEP
6

STEP
7

**STEP
8**

STEP
9

STEP
10

STEP
11

STEP
12

Key Signature

1 Flat

F Major

D Minor

The keys of F major and its relative,

D minor, have one flat.

FREE ACCESS on smartphones, iPhone, Android etc. Use any QR code app to scan this QR code

Or go straight to www.flametreemusic.com to **HEAR** chords, scales, and find more resources

162

STEP 8

Or go straight to www.flametreemusic.com to
HEAR chords, scales, and find more resources

Key Signature

2 Flats

B♭ Major

G Minor

The keys of B♭ major and its relative,

G minor, have two flats.

B♭ E♭

FREE ACCESS on smartphones, iPhone, Android etc.
Use any QR code app to scan this QR code

Or go straight to www.flametreemusic.com to
HEAR chords, scales, and find more resources

165

STEP
1

STEP
2

STEP
3

STEP
4

STEP
5

STEP
6

STEP
7

**STEP
8**

STEP
9

STEP
10

STEP
11

STEP
12

STEP
1

STEP
2

STEP
3

STEP
4

STEP
5

STEP
6

STEP
7

STEP
8

STEP
9

STEP
10

STEP
11

STEP
12

Key Signature

3 Flats

E♭ Major

C Minor

The keys of B♭ major and its relative,

G minor, have three flats:

B♭ E♭ A♭

FREE ACCESS on smartphones, iPhone, Android etc.
Use any QR code app to scan this QR code

Or go straight to www.flametreemusic.com to
HEAR chords, scales, and find more resources

166

FREE ACCESS on smartphones, iPhone, Android etc.
Use any QR code app to scan this QR code

Or go straight to www.flametreemusic.com to
HEAR chords, scales, and find more resources

STEP
1

STEP
2

STEP
3

STEP
4

STEP
5

STEP
6

STEP
7

**STEP
8**

STEP
9

STEP
10

STEP
11

STEP
12

STEP
1

STEP
2

STEP
3

STEP
4

STEP
5

STEP
6

STEP
7

STEP
8

STEP
9

STEP
10

STEP
11

STEP
12

Key Signature

4 Flats

A♭ Major

F Minor

The keys of A♭ major and its relative,

F minor, have four flats:

B♭ E♭ A♭ D♭

FREE ACCESS on smartphones, iPhone, Android etc.
Use any QR code app to scan this QR code

Or go straight to www.flametreemusic.com to
HEAR chords, scales, and find more resources

168

STEP 1

STEP 2

STEP 3

STEP 4

STEP 5

STEP 6

STEP 7

STEP 8

STEP 9

STEP 10

STEP 11

STEP 12

STEP 1
STEP 2
STEP 3
STEP 4
STEP 5
STEP 6
STEP 7
STEP 8
STEP 9
STEP 10
STEP 11
STEP 12

Key Signature

5 Flats

D♭ Major

B♭ Minor

The keys of D♭ major and its relative,

B♭ minor, have five flats:

B♭ E♭ A♭ D♭ G♭

FREE ACCESS on smartphones, iPhone, Android etc.
Use any QR code app to scan this QR code

Or go straight to www.flametreemusic.com to
HEAR chords, scales, and find more resources

170

FREE ACCESS on smartphones, iPhone, Android etc.
Use any QR code app to scan this QR code

Or go straight to www.flametreemusic.com to
HEAR chords, scales, and find more resources

STEP 1

STEP 2

STEP 3

STEP 4

STEP 5

STEP 6

STEP 7

STEP 8

STEP 9

STEP 10

STEP 11

STEP 12

STEP
1

STEP
2

STEP
3

STEP
4

STEP
5

STEP
6

STEP
7

STEP
8

STEP
9

STEP
10

STEP
11

STEP
12

Key Signature

6 Flats

G♭ Major

E♭ Minor

The keys of G♭ major and its relative,

E♭ minor, have six flats:

B♭ E♭ A♭ D♭ G♭ C♭

FREE ACCESS on smartphones, iPhone, Android etc.
Use any QR code app to scan this QR code

Or go straight to www.flametreemusic.com to
HEAR chords, scales, and find more resources

172

STEP
8

Or go straight to www.flametreemusic.com to
HEAR chords, scales, and find more resources

STEP
1

STEP
2

STEP
3

STEP
4

STEP
5

STEP
6

STEP
7

**STEP
8**

STEP
9

STEP
10

STEP
11

STEP
12

Key Signature

7 Flats

C♭ Major

A♭ Minor

The keys of C♭ major and its relative,

A♭ minor, have seven flats:

B♭ E♭ A♭ D♭ G♭ C♭ F♭

FREE ACCESS on smartphones, iPhone, Android etc. Use any QR code app to scan this QR code

Or go straight to www.flametreemusic.com to **HEAR** chords, scales, and find more resources

STEP 1
STEP 2
STEP 3
STEP 4
STEP 5
STEP 6
STEP 7
STEP 8
STEP 9
STEP 10
STEP 11
STEP 12

STEP 9

SCALES

Scales are rising and falling notes organized according to a particular pattern. All key signatures have major and harmonic minor scales associated with them, but there are other scales that allow further expression and are suitable for different types of music.

In this section we look at four scales per note: major, natural minor, harmonic minor, melodic minor. They each have a distinctive pattern which makes them suitable for a range of musical styles.

STEP
9

Or go straight to www.flametreemusic.com to **HEAR** chords, scales, and find more resources

STEP
1

STEP
2

STEP
3

STEP
4

STEP
5

STEP
6

STEP
7

STEP
8

STEP
9

STEP
10

STEP
11

STEP
12

Chromatic Scale

The simplest scale is the chromatic scale because it contains every note from the start to the end of an octave.

Every step of the scale is a **half tone**, or semitone.

Using middle C as the starting point, the C chromatic scale on the keyboard uses **every white** and every **black key** from C to the next C above.

The chromatic scale for every key works in the same way, taking in all the white and black keys, from the starting note of the key to the octave above.

FREE ACCESS on smartphones, iPhone, Android etc.
Use any QR code app to scan this QR code

Or go straight to www.flametreemusic.com to
HEAR chords, scales, and find more resources

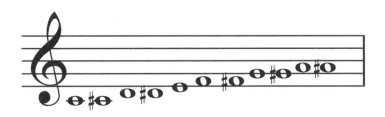

C C♯ D D♯ E F F♯ G G♯ A A♯ B

Piano: right hand fingering C chromatic scale.

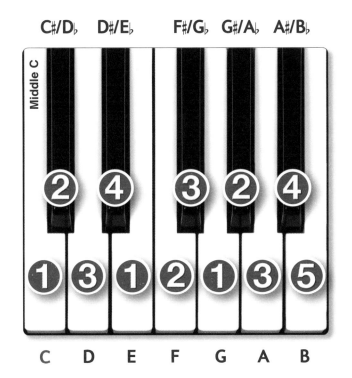

C♯/D♭ D♯/E♭ F♯/G♭ G♯/A♭ A♯/B♭

Middle C

② ④ ③ ② ④

① ③ ① ② ① ③ ⑤

C D E F G A B

1 thumb **2** index finger **3** middle finger **4** ring finger **5** little finger

Scale Patterns

This section show four scales for each note. Each scale conforms

to a standard pattern, from the root note of the scale.

S = semitone (half step); T = tone (whole step); m3 = minor 3rd (three semitones);

Major scale

T T S T T T S

Natural Minor

T S T T S T T

FREE ACCESS on smartphones, iPhone, Android etc.
Use any QR code app to scan this QR code

Or go straight to www.flametreemusic.com to
HEAR chords, scales, and find more resources

180

Harmonic Minor

T S T T S m3 S

Melodic Minor

T S T T T T S

(ascending form only)

Major Pentatonic

T T m3 T m3

Minor Pentatonic

m3 T T m3 T

STEP
9

STEP
10

FREE ACCESS on smartphones, iPhone, Android etc.
Use any QR code app to scan this QR code

Or go straight to www.flametreemusic.com to
HEAR chords, scales, and find more resources

181

STEP 1
STEP 2
STEP 3
STEP 4
STEP 5
STEP 6
STEP 7
STEP 8
STEP 9
STEP 10
STEP 11
STEP 12

C Major

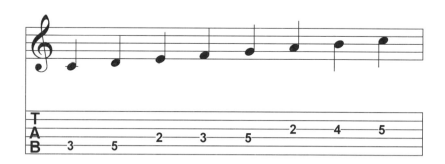

Scale notes	Up	C D E F G A B C
	down	C B A G F E D C

FREE ACCESS on smartphones, iPhone, Android etc.
Use any QR code app to scan this QR code

Or go straight to www.flametreemusic.com to
HEAR chords, scales, and find more resources

C Natural Minor

Scale notes	Up	C D E♭ F G A♭ B♭ C
	down	C B♭ A♭ G F E♭ D C

STEP 1

STEP 2

STEP 3

STEP 4

STEP 5

STEP 6

STEP 7

STEP 8

STEP 9

STEP 10

STEP 11

STEP 12

C Harmonic Minor

Scale notes	Up	C D E♭ F G A♭ B C
	down	C B A♭ G F E♭ D C

Or go straight to www.flametreemusic.com to **HEAR** chords, scales, and find more resources

C Melodic Minor

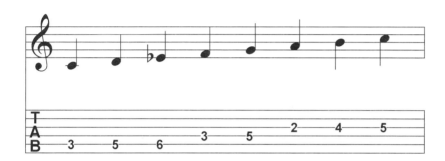

Scale notes	Up	C D E♭ F G A B C
	down	C B♭ A♭ G F E♭ D C

Or go straight to www.flametreemusic.com to
HEAR chords, scales, and find more resources

STEP
9

D♭ Major

Scale notes	Up	D♭ E♭ F G♭ A♭ B♭ C D♭
	down	D♭ C B♭ A♭ G♭ F E♭ D♭

FREE ACCESS on smartphones, iPhone, Android etc.
Use any QR code app to scan this QR code

Or go straight to www.flametreemusic.com to
HEAR chords, scales, and find more resources

186

C# Natural Minor

Scale notes	Up	C# D# E F# G# A B C#
	down	C# B A G# F# E D# C#

FREE ACCESS on smartphones, iPhone, Android etc. Use any QR code app to scan this QR code

187

Or go straight to www.flametreemusic.com to **HEAR** chords, scales, and find more resources

STEP 1
STEP 2
STEP 3
STEP 4
STEP 5
STEP 6
STEP 7
STEP 8
STEP 9
STEP 10
STEP 11
STEP 12

C# Harmonic Minor

Scale notes	Up	C# D# E F# G# A B# C#
	down	C# B# A G# F# E D# C#

FREE ACCESS on smartphones, iPhone, Android etc. Use any QR code app to scan this QR code

Or go straight to www.flametreemusic.com to **HEAR** chords, scales, and find more resources

C♯ Melodic Minor

Scale notes	Up	C♯ D♯ E F♯ G♯ A♯ B♯ C♯
	down	C♯ B♮ A♮ G♯ F♯ E D♯ C♯

Or go straight to www.flametreemusic.com to
HEAR chords, scales, and find more resources

D Major

Scale notes	Up	D E F♯ G A B C♯ D
	down	D C♯ B A G F♯ E D

FREE ACCESS on smartphones, iPhone, Android etc.
Use any QR code app to scan this QR code

Or go straight to www.flametreemusic.com to
HEAR chords, scales, and find more resources

190

D Natural Minor

Scale notes	Up	D E F G A B♭ C D
	down	D C B♭ A G F E D

FREE ACCESS on smartphones, iPhone, Android etc.
Use any QR code app to scan this QR code

Or go straight to www.flametreemusic.com to
HEAR chords, scales, and find more resources

191

STEP 1
STEP 2
STEP 3
STEP 4
STEP 5
STEP 6
STEP 7
STEP 8
STEP 9
STEP 10
STEP 11
STEP 12

STEP
1

STEP
2

STEP
3

STEP
4

STEP
5

STEP
6

STEP
7

STEP
8

**STEP
9**

STEP
10

STEP
11

STEP
12

D Harmonic Minor

Scale notes	Up	D E F G A B♭ C♯ D
	down	D C♯ B♭ A G F E D

FREE ACCESS on smartphones, iPhone, Android etc.
Use any QR code app to scan this QR code

Or go straight to www.flametreemusic.com to
HEAR chords, scales, and find more resources

D Melodic Minor

Scale notes	Up	D E F G A B C♯ D
	down	D C♮ B♭ A G F E D

STEP 1
STEP 2
STEP 3
STEP 4
STEP 5
STEP 6
STEP 7
STEP 8
STEP 9
STEP 10
STEP 11
STEP 12

FREE ACCESS on smartphones, iPhone, Android etc. Use any QR code app to scan this QR code

Or go straight to www.flametreemusic.com to **HEAR** chords, scales, and find more resources

193

E♭ Major

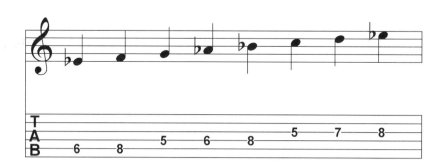

STEP 9

Scale notes	Up	E♭ F G A♭ B♭ C D E♭
	down	E♭ D C B♭ A♭ G F E♭

FREE ACCESS on smartphones, iPhone, Android etc.
Use any QR code app to scan this QR code

Or go straight to www.flametreemusic.com to
HEAR chords, scales, and find more resources

194

E♭ Natural Minor

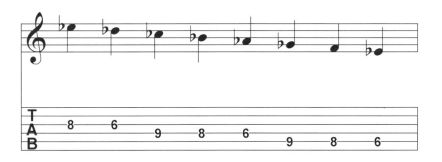

Scale notes	Up	E♭ F G♭ A♭ B♭ C♭ D♭ E♭
	down	E♭ D♭ C♭ B♭ A♭ G♭ F E♭

STEP
9

FREE ACCESS on smartphones, iPhone, Android etc.
Use any QR code app to scan this QR code

Or go straight to www.flametreemusic.com to
HEAR chords, scales, and find more resources

STEP 1
STEP 2
STEP 3
STEP 4
STEP 5
STEP 6
STEP 7
STEP 8
STEP 9
STEP 10
STEP 11
STEP 12

E♭ Harmonic Minor

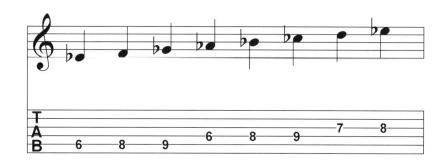

Scale notes	Up	E♭ F G♭ A♭ B♭ C♭ D E♭
	down	E♭ D C♭ B♭ A♭ G♭ F E♭

FREE ACCESS on smartphones, iPhone, Android etc. Use any QR code app to scan this QR code

Or go straight to www.flametreemusic.com to **HEAR** chords, scales, and find more resources

196

E♭ Melodic Minor

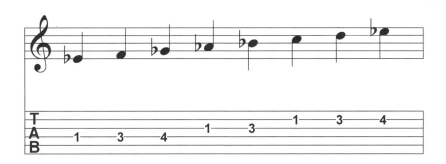

Scale notes	Up	E♭ F G♭ A♭ B♭ C D E♭
	down	E♭ D♭ C♭ B♭ A♭ G♭ F E♭

Or go straight to www.flametreemusic.com to
HEAR chords, scales, and find more resources

STEP 1
STEP 2
STEP 3
STEP 4
STEP 5
STEP 6
STEP 7
STEP 8
STEP 9
STEP 10
STEP 11
STEP 12

E Major

Scale notes	Up	E F♯ G♯ A B C♯ D♯ E
	down	E D♯ C♯ B A G♯ F♯ E

E Natural Minor

Scale notes	Up	E F♯ G A B C D E
	down	E D C B A G F♯ E

FREE ACCESS on smartphones, iPhone, Android etc. Use any QR code app to scan this QR code

Or go straight to www.flametreemusic.com to **HEAR** chords, scales, and find more resources

E Harmonic Minor

Scale notes	Up	E F# G A B C D# E
	down	E D# C B A G F# E

FREE ACCESS on smartphones, iPhone, Android etc.
Use any QR code app to scan this QR code

Or go straight to www.flametreemusic.com to **HEAR** chords, scales, and find more resources

E Melodic Minor

Scale notes	Up	E F♯ G A B C♯ D♯ E
	down	E D♮ C♮ B A G F♯ E

Or go straight to www.flametreemusic.com to
HEAR chords, scales, and find more resources

F Major

Scale notes	Up	F G A B♭ C D E F
	down	F E D C B♭ A G F

FREE ACCESS on smartphones, iPhone, Android etc. Use any QR code app to scan this QR code

Or go straight to www.flametreemusic.com to **HEAR** chords, scales, and find more resources

202

STEP 9

F Natural Minor

STEP
9

Scale notes Up   F G A♭ B♭ C D♭ E♭ F
           down F E♭ D♭ C B♭ A♭ G F

FREE ACCESS on smartphones, iPhone, Android etc.
Use any QR code app to scan this QR code

Or go straight to www.flametreemusic.com to
HEAR chords, scales, and find more resources

203

F Harmonic Minor

Scale notes	Up	F G A♭ B♭ C D♭ E F
	down	F E D♭ C B♭ A♭ G F

FREE ACCESS on smartphones, iPhone, Android etc.
Use any QR code app to scan this QR code

Or go straight to www.flametreemusic.com to
HEAR chords, scales, and find more resources

F Melodic Minor

Scale notes	Up	F G A♭ B♭ C D E F
	down	F E♭ D♭ C B♭ A♭ G F

Or go straight to www.flametreemusic.com to
HEAR chords, scales, and find more resources

F♯ Major

Scale notes

Up F♯ G♯ A♯ B C♯ D♯ E♯ F♯

down F♯ E♯ D♯ C♯ B A♯ G♯ F♯

F♯ Natural Minor

Scale notes	Up	F♯ G♯ A B C♯ D E F♯
	down	F♯ E D C♯ B A G♯ F♯

STEP 1
STEP 2
STEP 3
STEP 4
STEP 5
STEP 6
STEP 7
STEP 8
STEP 9
STEP 10
STEP 11
STEP 12

F♯ Harmonic Minor

Scale notes
Up F♯ G♯ A B C♯ D E♯ F♯
down F♯ E♯ D C♯ B A G♯ F♯

F# Melodic Minor

Scale notes	Up	F# G# A B C# D# E# F#
	down	F# E♮ D♮ C# B A G# F#

FREE ACCESS on smartphones, iPhone, Android etc. Use any QR code app to scan this QR code

Or go straight to www.flametreemusic.com to **HEAR** chords, scales, and find more resources

209

STEP 1
STEP 2
STEP 3
STEP 4
STEP 5
STEP 6
STEP 7
STEP 8
STEP 9
STEP 10
STEP 11
STEP 12

G Major

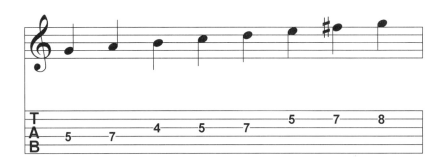

Scale notes	Up	G A B C D E F♯ G
	down	G F♯ E D C B A G

G Natural Minor

Scale notes	Up	G A B♭ C D E♭ F G
	down	G F E♭ D C B♭ A G

Or go straight to www.flametreemusic.com to **HEAR** chords, scales, and find more resources

STEP 9

G Harmonic Minor

Scale notes	Up	G A B♭ C D E♭ F♯ G
	down	G F♯ E♭ D C B♭ A G

FREE ACCESS on smartphones, iPhone, Android etc.
Use any QR code app to scan this QR code

Or go straight to www.flametreemusic.com to
HEAR chords, scales, and find more resources

212

G Melodic Minor

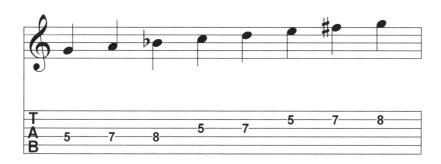

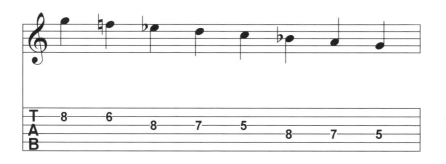

Scale notes	Up	G A B♭ C D E F♯ G
	down	G F♮ E♭ D C B♭ A G

FREE ACCESS on smartphones, iPhone, Android etc.
Use any QR code app to scan this QR code

Or go straight to www.flametreemusic.com to
HEAR chords, scales, and find more resources

STEP 1
STEP 2
STEP 3
STEP 4
STEP 5
STEP 6
STEP 7
STEP 8
STEP 9
STEP 10
STEP 11
STEP 12

A♭ Major

Scale notes

Up A♭ B♭ C D♭ E♭ F G A♭
down A♭ G F E♭ D♭ C B♭ A♭

Or go straight to www.flametreemusic.com to
HEAR chords, scales, and find more resources

STEP
9

G♯ Natural Minor

Scale notes

Up   G♯ A♯ B C♯ D♯ E F♯ G♯

down   G♯ F♯ E D♯ C♯ B A♯ G♯

FREE ACCESS on smartphones, iPhone, Android etc. Use any QR code app to scan this QR code

Or go straight to www.flametreemusic.com to **HEAR** chords, scales, and find more resources

STEP 9

G♯ Harmonic Minor

This double sharp symbol raises the note by two semitones.

Scale notes	Up	G♯ A♯ B C♯ D♯ E F× G♯
	down	G♯ F× E D♯ C♯ B A♯ G♯

G♯ Melodic Minor

This double sharp symbol raises the note by two semitones.

Scale notes	Up	G♯ A♯ B C♯ D♯ E F× G♯
	down	G♯ F× E D♯ C♯ B A♯ G♯

Or go straight to www.flametreemusic.com to **HEAR** chords, scales, and find more resources

STEP 1
STEP 2
STEP 3
STEP 4
STEP 5
STEP 6
STEP 7
STEP 8
STEP 9
STEP 10
STEP 11
STEP 12

A Major

STEP
9

Scale notes	Up	C D E F G A B C
	down	C B A G F E D C

FREE ACCESS on smartphones, iPhone, Android etc.
Use any QR code app to scan this QR code

Or go straight to www.flametreemusic.com to
HEAR chords, scales, and find more resources

A Natural Minor

STEP
9

Scale notes	Up	A B C D E F G A
	down	A G F E D C B A

A Harmonic Minor

Scale notes	Up	A B C D E F G# A
	down	A G# F E D C B A

A Melodic Minor

Scale notes	Up	A B C D E F♯ G♯ A
	down	A G♮ F♮ E D C B A

FREE ACCESS on smartphones, iPhone, Android etc.
Use any QR code app to scan this QR code

Or go straight to www.flametreemusic.com to
HEAR chords, scales, and find more resources

221

STEP 1
STEP 2
STEP 3
STEP 4
STEP 5
STEP 6
STEP 7
STEP 8
STEP 9
STEP 10
STEP 11
STEP 12

B♭ Major

Scale notes	Up	B♭ C D E♭ F G A B♭
	down	B♭ A G F E♭ D C B♭

STEP
9

B♭ Natural Minor

Scale notes	Up	B♭ C D♭ E♭ F G♭ A♭ B♭
	down	B♭ A♭ G♭ F E♭ D♭ C B♭

FREE ACCESS on smartphones, iPhone, Android etc.
Use any QR code app to scan this QR code

Or go straight to www.flametreemusic.com to
HEAR chords, scales, and find more resources

223

STEP
9

B♭ Harmonic Minor

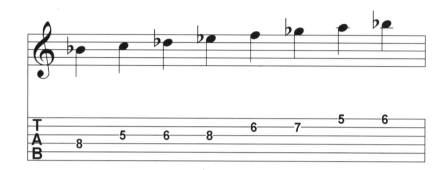

Scale notes	Up	B♭ C D♭ E♭ F G♭ A B♭
	down	B♭ A G♭ F E♭ D♭ C B♭

FREE ACCESS on smartphones, iPhone, Android etc.
Use any QR code app to scan this QR code

Or go straight to www.flametreemusic.com to
HEAR chords, scales, and find more resources

224

B♭ Melodic Minor

Scale notes	Up	B♭ C D♭ E♭ F G A B♭
	down	B♭ A♭ G♭ F E♭ D♭ C B♭

STEP 1
STEP 2
STEP 3
STEP 4
STEP 5
STEP 6
STEP 7
STEP 8
STEP 9
STEP 10
STEP 11
STEP 12

B Major

Scale notes		
	Up	B C♯ D♯ E F♯ G♯ A♯ B
	down	B A♯ G♯ F♯ E D♯ C♯ B

FREE ACCESS on smartphones, iPhone, Android etc. Use any QR code app to scan this QR code

Or go straight to www.flametreemusic.com to **HEAR** chords, scales, and find more resources

226

B Natural Minor

Scale notes	Up	B C# D E F# G A B
	down	B A G F# E D C# B

STEP 9

Or go straight to www.flametreemusic.com to **HEAR** chords, scales, and find more resources

B Harmonic Minor

| **Scale notes** | Up | B C♯ D E F♯ G A♯ B |
| | down | B A♯ G F♯ E D C♯ B |

FREE ACCESS on smartphones, iPhone, Android etc.
Use any QR code app to scan this QR code

228

Or go straight to www.flametreemusic.com to
HEAR chords, scales, and find more resources

B Melodic Minor

Scale notes	Up	B C# D E F# G# A# B
	down	B A♮ G♮ F# E D C# B

Or go straight to www.flametreemusic.com to
HEAR chords, scales, and find more resources

STEP 1
STEP 2
STEP 3
STEP 4
STEP 5
STEP 6
STEP 7
STEP 8
STEP 9
STEP 10
STEP 11
STEP 12

STEP 10

CHORDS FROM SCALES

We've looked at single notes played one at a time, so now its time to move on to chords, which can be used to accompany single-line melodies. Chords add richness and depth to music and can be played on any instrument capable of making more than one sound at a time: such as keyboard, guitar, or harp. For rock, blues and folk musicians chords often provide the backbone to their songwriting. Melodic instruments and voices joined together also create a chord-like sound, with many melodies joining in a series of chord-like structures.

STEP
10

FREE ACCESS on smartphones, iPhone, Android etc. Use any QR code app to scan this QR code

Or go straight to www.flametreemusic.com to **HEAR** chords, scales, and find more resources

231

How to Make a Chord from a Scale

STEP 1
STEP 2
STEP 3
STEP 4
STEP 5
STEP 6
STEP 7
STEP 8
STEP 9
STEP 10
STEP 11
STEP 12

If you know which key to start in, you can identify which chords will work in that key.

Simple chords are called **triads** because they are made up of **three notes**.

To find the simple triad chords from a scale, use **any note** within to **start**, then **add** the **note two up**, then **add** the note **two up again**.

The **root** note of a chord is the **lowest** note: for example, the C major chord will have C as its root, and D major will have D as its root.

FREE ACCESS on smartphones, iPhone, Android etc.
Use any QR code app to scan this QR code

Or go straight to www.flametreemusic.com to
HEAR chords, scales, and find more resources

232

C Major Scale

C	D	E	F	G	A	B	C
1st	2nd	3rd	4th	5th	6th	7th octave	
I	II	III	IV	V	VI	VII	

C Major chord

1st + 3rd + 5th notes of the C Major scale

G
E
C

↑
Root note

F Major chord

4th + 6th + octave notes of the C Major scale

C
A
F

↑
Root note

G Major chord

5th + 7th + high 2nd notes of the C Major scale

D
B
G

↑
Root note

STEP 1
STEP 2
STEP 3
STEP 4
STEP 5
STEP 6
STEP 7
STEP 8
STEP 9
STEP 10
STEP 11
STEP 12

FREE ACCESS on smartphones, iPhone, Android etc. Use any QR code app to scan this QR code

Or go straight to www.flametreemusic.com to **HEAR** chords, scales, and find more resources

233

Chord Inversions

A chord that has a bottom note other than its root note is called an inverted chord.

Inverted chords are used to add colour and variety to a musical piece. A bass or double bass might play the root notes while the keyboard or string players might play an inverted chord above the root note.

As an example, the C major chord can be played with the **root note** of **C**, or the **E** or the **G**.

STEP
10

FREE ACCESS on smartphones, iPhone, Android etc.
Use any QR code app to scan this QR code

Or go straight to www.flametreemusic.com to
HEAR chords, scales, and find more resources

234

C Major Scale

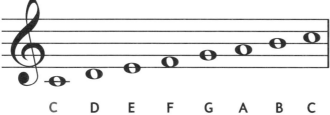

C	D	E	F	G	A	B	C
1st	2nd	3rd	4th	5th	6th	7th	octave
I	II	III	IV	V	VI	VII	

C Major chord

1st, 3rd and 5th notes
of the C Major scale

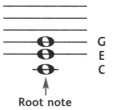

G
E
C

↑
Root note

C Major 1st Inversion

3rd and 5th and octave notes
of the C Major scale

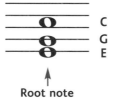

C
G
E

↑
Root note

C Major 2nd Inversion

5th, octave and high 3rd notes
of the C Major scale

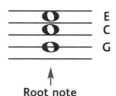

E
C
G

↑
Root note

STEP
10

FREE ACCESS on smartphones, iPhone, Android etc. Use any QR code app to scan this QR code

Or go straight to www.flametreemusic.com to **HEAR** chords, scales, and find more resources

Common Chords of the
C Major Scale

STEP 1
STEP 2
STEP 3
STEP 4
STEP 5
STEP 6
STEP 7
STEP 8
STEP 9
STEP 10
STEP 11
STEP 12

Notes

C	D	E	F	G	A	B
I	II	III	IV	V	VI	VII

Chord IV

IV, VI, I

F Major

Notes: F, A, C

Chord I

I, III, V

C Major

Notes: C, E, G

Chord V

V, VII, II

G Major

Notes: G, B, D

Chord II

II, IV, VI

D Minor

Notes: D, F, A

Chord VI

VI, I, III

A Minor

Notes: A, C, E

Common Chords of the
D♭ Major Scale

Notes

D♭	E♭	F	G♭	A♭	B♭	C
I	II	III	IV	V	VI	VII

Chord IV

IV, VI, I

G♭ Major

Notes: G♭, B♭, D♭

Chord I

I, III, V

D♭ Major

Notes: D♭, F, A♭

Chord V

V, VII, II

A♭ Major

Notes: A♭, C, E♭

Chord II

II, IV, VI

E♭ Minor

Notes: E♭, G♭, B♭

Chord VI

VI, I, III

B♭ Minor

Notes: B♭, D♭, F

STEP 1

STEP 2

STEP 3

STEP 4

STEP 5

STEP 6

STEP 7

STEP 8

STEP 9

STEP 10

STEP 11

STEP 12

FREE ACCESS on smartphones, iPhone, Android etc. Use any QR code app to scan this QR code

Or go straight to www.flametreemusic.com to **HEAR** chords, scales, and find more resources

237

Common Chords of the
D Major Scale

Notes						
D	E	F♯	G	A	B	C♯
I	II	III	IV	V	VI	VII

Chord IV
IV, VI, I
G Major
Notes: G, B, D

Chord I
I, III, V
D Major
Notes: D, F♯, A

Chord V
V, VII, II
A Major
Notes: A, C♯, E

Chord II
II, IV, VI
E Minor
Notes: E, G, B

Chord VI
VI, I, III
B Minor
Notes: B, D, F♯

STEP
10

FREE ACCESS on smartphones, iPhone, Android etc. Use any QR code app to scan this QR code

Or go straight to www.flametreemusic.com to **HEAR** chords, scales, and find more resources

Common Chords of the
E♭ Major Scale

Notes

E♭	F	G	A♭	B♭	C	D
I	II	III	IV	V	VI	VII

Chord IV

IV, VI, I

A♭ Major

Notes: A♭, C, E♭

Chord I

I, III, V

E♭ Major

Notes: E♭, G, B♭

Chord V

V, VII, II

B♭ Major

Notes: B♭, D, F

Chord II

II, IV, VI

F Minor

Notes: F, A♭, C

Chord VI

VI, I, III

C Minor

Notes: C, E♭, G

FREE ACCESS on smartphones, iPhone, Android etc. Use any QR code app to scan this QR code  Or go straight to www.flametreemusic.com to **HEAR** chords, scales, and find more resources

239

STEP 10

Common Chords of the
E Major Scale

STEP 1
STEP 2
STEP 3
STEP 4
STEP 5
STEP 6
STEP 7
STEP 8
STEP 9
STEP 10
STEP 11
STEP 12

Notes

E	F♯	G♯	A	B	C♯	D♯
I	II	III	IV	V	VI	VII

Chord IV

IV, VI, I

A Major

Notes: A, C♯, E

Chord I

I, III, V

E Major

Notes: E, G♯, B

Chord V

V, VII, II

B Major

Notes: B, D♯, F♯

Chord II

II, IV, VI

F♯ Minor

Notes: F♯, A, C♯

Chord VI

VI, I, III

C♯ Minor

Notes: C♯, E, G♯

FREE ACCESS on smartphones, iPhone, Android etc. Use any QR code app to scan this QR code

Or go straight to www.flametreemusic.com to **HEAR** chords, scales, and find more resources

Common Chords of the
F Major Scale

Notes

F	G	A	Bb	C	D	E
I	II	III	IV	V	VI	VII

Chord IV

IV, VI, I

Bb Major

Notes: Bb, D, F

Chord I

I, III, V

F Major

Notes: F, A, C

Chord V

V, VII, II

C Major

Notes: C, E, G

Chord II

II, IV, VI

G Minor

Notes: G, Bb, D

Chord VI

VI, I, III

D Minor

Notes: D, F, A

STEP
10

Common Chords of the
F♯ Major Scale

Notes						
F♯	G♯	A♯	B	C♯	D♯	E♯
I	II	III	IV	V	VI	VII

Chord IV

IV, VI, I

B Major

Notes: B, D♯, F♯

Chord I

I, III, V

F♯ Major

Notes: F♯, A♯, C♯

Chord V

V, VII, II

C♯ Major

Notes: C♯, E♯, G♯

Chord II

II, IV, VI

G♯ Minor

Notes: G♯, B, D♯

Chord VI

VI, I, III

D♯ Minor

Notes: D♯, F♯, A♯

STEP 10

Common Chords of the
G Major Scale

Notes

G	A	B	C	D	E	F♯
I	II	III	IV	V	VI	VII

Chord IV

IV, VI, I

C Major

Notes: C, E, G

Chord I

I, III, V

G Major

Notes: G, B, D

Chord V

V, VII, II

D Major

Notes: D, F♯, A

Chord II

II, IV, VI

A Minor

Notes: A, C, E

Chord VI

VI, I, III

E Minor

Notes: E, G, B

STEP 10

FREE ACCESS on smartphones, iPhone, Android etc.
Use any QR code app to scan this QR code

Or go straight to www.flametreemusic.com to
HEAR chords, scales, and find more resources

243

Common Chords of the
A♭ Major Scale

Notes						
A♭	B♭	C	D♭	E♭	F	G
I	II	III	IV	V	VI	VII

Chord IV
IV, VI, I

D♭ Major

Notes: D♭, F, A♭

Chord I
I, III, V

A♭ Major

Notes: A♭, C, E♭

Chord V
V, VII, II

E♭ Major

Notes: E♭, G, B♭

Chord II
II, IV, VI

B♭ Minor

Notes: B♭, D♭, F

Chord VI
VI, I, III

F Minor

Notes: F, A♭, C

STEP 1
STEP 2
STEP 3
STEP 4
STEP 5
STEP 6
STEP 7
STEP 8
STEP 9
STEP 10
STEP 11
STEP 12

Common Chords of the
A Major Scale

Notes						
A	B	C♯	D	E	F♯	G♯
I	II	III	IV	V	VI	VII

Chord IV

IV, VI, I

D Major

Notes: D, F♯, A

Chord I

I, III, V

A Major

Notes: A, C♯, E

Chord V

V, VII, II

E Major

Notes: E, G♯, B

Chord II

II, IV, VI

B Minor

Notes: B, D, F♯

Chord VI

VI, I, III

F♯ Minor

Notes: F♯, A, C♯

STEP 1
STEP 2
STEP 3
STEP 4
STEP 5
STEP 6
STEP 7
STEP 8
STEP 9
STEP 10
STEP 11
STEP 12

Common Chords of the
B♭ Major Scale

Notes

B♭	C	D	E♭	F	G	A
I	II	III	IV	V	VI	VII

Chord IV

IV, VI, I

E♭ Major

Notes: E♭, G, B♭

Chord I

I, III, V

B♭ Major

Notes: B♭, D, F

Chord V

V, VII, II

F Major

Notes: F, A, C

Chord II

II, IV, VI

C Minor

Notes: C, E♭, G

Chord VI

VI, I, III

G Minor

Notes: G, B♭, D

Or go straight to www.flametreemusic.com to **HEAR** chords, scales, and find more resources

STEP 10

Common Chords of the
B Major Scale

Notes

B	C♯	D♯	E	F♯	G♯	A♯
I	II	III	IV	V	VI	VII

Chord IV

IV, VI, I

E Major

Notes: E, G♯, B

Chord I

I, III, V

B Major

Notes: B, D♯, F♯

Chord V

V, VII, II

F♯ Major

Notes: F♯, A♯, C♯

Chord II

II, IV, VI

C♯ Minor

Notes: C♯, E, G♯

Chord VI

VI, I, III

G♯ Minor

Notes: G♯, B, D♯

STEP
10

FREE ACCESS on smartphones, iPhone, Android etc. Use any QR code app to scan this QR code

Or go straight to www.flametreemusic.com to **HEAR** chords, scales, and find more resources

STEP 11

SYMBOLS & MARKS

A musical piece is often full of symbols, all of which provide clues about how the music should be played: how loud, what speed and when to repeat.

Classical music uses a great many Italian terms because in the early 1600s Italy was the cultural centre of European music. Church choral music moved to broader orchestral forms, the major and minor scales were standardized and tonal music gained great influence, resulting in the western classical style. The twentieth century brought an explosion of new styles of music (blues, jazz, rock) and with them the greater use of English terms.

STEP
11

FREE ACCESS on smartphones, iPhone, Android etc. Use any QR code app to scan this QR code

Or go straight to www.flametreemusic.com to **HEAR** chords, scales, and find more resources

249

STEP
11

Tempo

These marks are written above the music and show how quickly to play the music.

lento or *adagio*	slowly
andante	at walking speed
moderato	moderate speed
allegretto	fairly fast
allegro	fast
presto	very fast
ritardando (rit.)	slowing down
accelerando (accel.)	getting faster
a tempo	at original speed
piu mosso	faster
meno mosso	slower
ad lib./ad libitum	freely

Dynamics

These marks are written below the notes and show how loudly to play the music.

pp	*pianissimo*	very quiet
p	*piano*	quiet
mp	*mezzopiano*	fairly quiet

mf	*mezzoforte*	fairly loud
f	*forte*	loud
ff	*fortissimo*	very loud
<	*crescendo (cresc.)*	growing louder
>	*diminuendo (dim.)*	growing quieter

Articulation

These marks are written above or below the notes and show how to play the notes.

.	*staccato*	short
>	*accento*	accented
ʌ	*marcato*	louder accent
_	*tenuto*	slightly stressed
⌒	*legato*	slur, smooth
sfz	*sforzando*	forced, heavy accent
fp	*fortepiano*	loud attack then quiet
⌢	*fermata*	hold, pause
8va	*all' ottava*	One octave higher than written
8ab.	*ottava bassa*	One octave lower than written
tr	∿∿∿∿∿∿	trill

Other Symbols

D.C. al Fine	Return to the beginning and play to ***Fine*** (end).
D.S. al Fine	Return to and play to ***Fine.***
D.C. al Coda	Return to the beginning, play to ⊕ and skip to Coda.
D.S. al Coda	Return to , play to ⊕ and skip to Coda.

 Return to the beginning or nearest repeat sign.

Stems and Beams

Notes **below** the **third line** are written with their **stems up**.

For **beamed notes**, the note furthest from the third line determines the stem direction.

STEP 11

STEP 12

GOING ONLINE

Finally, you can go to www.flametreemusic.com
where you can find and listen to chords,
scales and other resources to help
you learn more as a musician.

FREE ACCESS on smartphones, iPhone, Android etc.
Use any QR code app to scan this QR code

Or go straight to www.flametreemusic.com to
HEAR chords, scales, and find more resources

253

FlameTreeMusic.com gives you a number of resources to complement this book:

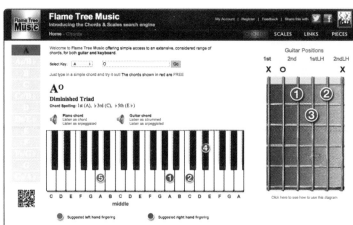

- A wide range of chords which can be **heard** in piano and guitar sounds.
- 20 core scales are provided for each key, again you can **hear** the notes played on the guitar and the piano.

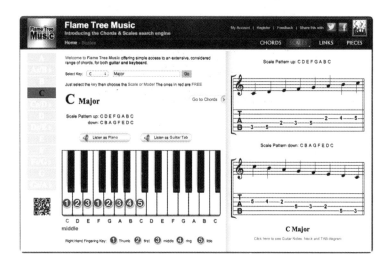

FREE ACCESS on smartphones, iPhone, Android etc.
Use any QR code app to scan this QR code

Or go straight to www.flametreemusic.com to
HEAR chords, scales, and find more resources

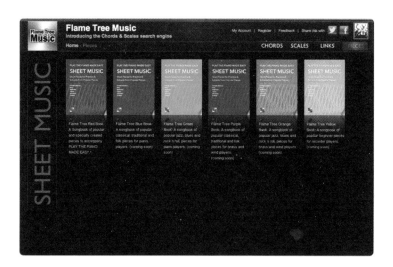

- **The Flame Tree Red book** offers over 100 pages of popular tunes and examples for the piano. It can be viewed online using a desktop computer, on a tablet such as an iPad, or on a smartphone such as an iPhone. Other books offer different selections of pieces for the piano and a variety of wind instruments.

- Other resources on the site include **links** and **book recommendations** to extend your knowledge. There are a great many excellent publications available, both in print and increasingly online. We'll update this resource frequently.

We're always looking for ways to improve what we do so please give us feedback on our Facebook page. ⨍ www.facebook.com/flametreemusic.

FREE ACCESS on smartphones, iPhone, Android etc. Use any QR code app to scan this QR code

Or go straight to www.flametreemusic.com to **HEAR** chords, scales, and find more resources

STEP
12

READING MUSIC MADE EASY

A new title in our best-selling series, designed for players of all ages. Created for musicians by musicians, these books offer a quick and practical resource for those playing on their own or with a band. They work equally well for the rock and indie musician as they do for the jazz, folk, country, blues or classical enthusiast.

The MUSIC MADE EASY series
See it and Hear it! Comprehensive sound links
Guitar Chords Made Easy, Piano and Keyboard Chords Made Easy, Scales and Modes Made Easy, Reading Music Made Easy, Play the Piano Made Easy, Play the Guitar Made Easy.

The SPIRAL, EASY-TO-USE series
Advanced Guitar Chords; Advanced Piano Chords; Guitar Chords; Piano & Keyboard Chords; Chords for Kids; Play Flamenco; How to Play Guitar; How to Play Bass Guitar; How to Play Classic Riffs; Songwriter's Rhyming Dictionary; How to Become a Star; How to Read Music; How to Write Great Songs; How to Play Rock Rhythm, Riffs & Lead; How to Play Hard, Metal & Nu Rock; How to Make Music on the Web; My First Recorder Music; Piano Sheet Music; Brass & Wind Sheet Music; Scales & Modes; Beginners' Guide to Reading Music

For further information on these titles please visit our trading website:
www.flametreepublishing.com

www.flametreemusic.com
Practical information on chords, scales, riffs, rhymes and instruments through a growing combination of traditional print books and ebooks. Features over **1800 chords** and **240 scales** with **sound files** for notes and strummed chords.

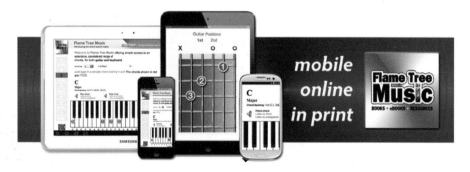